AF147909

What Larks

Collected ^light^ verse and lyrics

by

Jeremy Nicholas

First published February 2022
978 1 913089 58 0
Published by Porter Press International Ltd
Hilltop Farm, Knighton-on-Teme,
Tenbury Wells, WR15 8LY, UK
Tel: +44 (0)1584 781588
sales@porterpress.co.uk
www.porterpress.co.uk

Edited by Philip Porter
Design & illustrations by Martin Port
Printed by Gomer Press Ltd

Porter Press International

For Jillie – 40 years on

Contents

Foreword
by Sir Tim Rice

I have known and admired Jeremy Nicholas's work for many years and it is about time that selections of his creations were all gathered together in one place. Now is the time and this is the place.

As a lyricist the words assembled herein demonstrate his indisputable dexterity; where he has one over me and many other pliers of my trade is that he writes music as well. You will have to search elsewhere for that but fortunately the jocularity and skill with which his words are imbued will be more than enough to make you feel you have not forked out in vain for this distinguished tome.

Unlike some in the murkier departments of the trade today, Jeremy makes sure his stuff rhymes and scans, although in his autobiographical introduction he is not ashamed to expose his early shortcomings in those disciplines, essential above all for the humorous songwriter. Today, like me, he would not dream of using two syllables where only one is required. Unless there was a panic deadline of course.

Whether he is warbling them himself, or whether others are giving voice to his wit and wisdom, it is always a pleasure to listen to his rhyme and reason. It is also a pleasure simply to read them as the following pages will confirm.

Tim Rice
February 2022
Near exit 4 on the M40

Introduction

The rhythm of words, a perfectly-placed punchline, an ingenious rhyming scheme – all appealed to me at a very early age. Much later I realised what a satisfying way it was to make people laugh with… well, what is it to be called? Light verse? Humorous verse? Comic verse? Looking back, it was probably the random recordings in my parents' collection that got me started – and a poem that my mother recited over and over again, long before I had learned to read. I have never discovered who wrote it, but it was one that she had learnt from her own mother before the First World War.

> Mr Archibald McCann was an absent-minded man
> In fact, he never knew what he was at.
> In the morning he arose and went and washed his clothes
> And hung himself upon the line to dry.
> The neighbours said, 'Good gracious! This certainly is vexatious!'
> As they heard the people laughing passing by.
> He gave his dinner meat to the puppy dog to eat
> And ate the bones himself upon the mat.
> But this would not have mattered if the servants hadn't chattered,
> And then he vowed he'd growl to scare the cat.
> He wrote a note one day to his brother, far away,
> And fell inside the post-box through the slit.
> So perhaps he's gone to Russia, Turkey, France or Prussia.
> I shouldn't be surprised a little bit.

In my parents' library were copies of Mother Goose, Lewis Carroll, Edward Lear and Hilaire Belloc. Among the collection of recordings was a 9-inch 78rpm disc of a Swiss yodeller called Fred Farelli. Side 1 had *The Yodelling Mountaineer*. At the age of four or five I thought some of the rhymes were terribly funny:

One day he climbed a mountain and was singing in the snow
When from the top he fell down plop but still sang on below…
On the day he passed away, he lay in his socks
And yodelled just before they gently put him in his box…

Also stored in the front of the Murphy radiogram were two early LPs of the D'Oyly Carte Opera Company in *The Mikado*, conducted by Isadore Godfrey. Gilbert's lyrics married to Sullivan's stream of effortless melody took hold of me. I knew it all by the time I was seven – 'A wandering minstrel I', 'I've got him on the list', 'A more humane Mikado', and…

The flowers that bloom in the spring (tra-lah)
Have nothing to do with the case (tra-lah)
And I've got to take under my wing (tra-lah)
A most unattractive old thing (tra-lah)
With a caricature of a face.

Parodies particularly appealed and I quickly progressed from

Oh dear what can the matter be,
Three old ladies were locked in the lavatory.

and

While shepherds watched the box at night
All tuned to ITV,
The angel of the Lord came down
And changed to BBC.

to the more risqué

They're changing sex at Buckingham Palace –
Christopher Robin turned into Alice.

and

Puff the Magic Dragon
Lived on a shelf
He didn't have no playmates, so
Puff played with himself.

Parallel to my growing (and lifelong) addiction to classical music was a diet of Flanders and Swann, Paddy Roberts, Noël Coward, and Stanley Holloway, many of whose famous monologues, such as *The Lion and Albert*, were written by the incomparable Marriot Edgar. There was also, let me not forget, a huge repertoire of schoolboy filth and rugby songs. All of these greatly attracted me – as long as they scanned, rhymed and made me laugh.

I began writing my own stuff. During prep in the Senior School one evening, I came up with this, a parody of 'There is nothing like a dame' from *South Pacific*.

We've got toilets, we've got drains
We're connected to the mains,
We've got white enamel pedestals
You flush by pulling chains,
And you sometimes get a broken hook
To hang up all your caper.
What don't you get?
You don't get paper!

I consider this essential
To basic human needs
For the lack of this commodity
To many problems leads.

> For if you do not have the stuff
> To use just as you please
> Guess what you get?
> Venereal disease.

A pity about the extra syllables in the antepenultimate and final lines of verse one. The repetition of 'For' in the second verse is not good either, but on the whole it was not a bad early effort, though how you contract VD from not having toilet paper I'm not sure.

Other influences: another 78rpm disc somehow found its way into my parents' collection, far too near the knuckle for them: *They have a much better time when they're naughty* sung by Ronald Frankau, 'The Blue Boy of Variety'. The final verse was pushing it, even for Frankau, and especially for the Parlophone label:

> The good girl takes an omnibus and pays her penny fare.
> The bad girl takes a taxi – and you know what happens there!
> The good girl has a geyser with a penny in or more.
> The bad girl has a marble bath and doesn't lock the door.

> [Then, spoken by Frankau after the final chorus]:

> The good girl likes the light on and hopes she'll have some luck.
> The bad girl turns the light out and hopes the man has pluck…

After I became an actor, there were some long-forgotten revues to which I contributed, and an ill-fated musical about the actress Sarah Bernhardt entitled *Sarah B. Divine* for which I provided music and lyrics.

By then, I had become immersed in the Great American Songbook – the Gershwins, Cole Porter, Berlin, Harry Warren and Al Dubin, Rodgers and Hart, Rodgers and Hammerstein and others, with their elegant, literate lyrics and unforgettable melodies – and the songs of the British Music Hall and Variety: Max Miller, Leslie Sarony, Noel Gay, The Western Brothers, Billy Bennett and many more who could fashion a laugh out of a clever rhyme.

Then there was the incomparable Tom Lehrer – dead-pan, subversive and unpredictable:

'Take your cigarette from its holder
And burn your initials in my shoulder'
(The Masochism Tango)

'Do whatever steps you want if
You have cleared them with the Pontiff.
Everybody say his own
Kyrie eleison
Doin' the Vatican Rag.
(The Vatican Rag)

Writing lyrics and music was very much a hobby until 1975 when my acting work brought me into contact with the singer/songwriter Peter Skellern. Through him, I began writing topical and/or humorous songs for a programme called *Stop the Week* on BBC Radio 4. That was when I started to take comic verse seriously. There is more on this later in the book.

With the help of Clement Wood's indispensable *Unabridged Rhyming Dictionary* (the best £10.50 I ever spent) and stimulated by the challenges of writing for *Stop the Week*, I explored other outlets. First, I had the idea of writing a modern parody of Hilaire Belloc's *Cautionary Tales*. I called it *Raspberries and Other Trifles*. It was published in 1984 with wonderful illustrations by Jon Higham, then just out of art college. My mother, to whom the book is dedicated, went to her local branch of W H Smith to order some copies for friends. She found it in the cookery section.

The next project was more ambitious: a rhyming history of Britain – or, to be more precise, all the Kings and Queens of England and the United Kingdom, from Canute to the present day. It is entitled *A Throne of Your Own*. Alas, having got as far as King John and unable to find a publisher, I abandoned it. This was followed by new verses for Saint Saëns's *The Carnival of the Animals* and various other projects, all of which are published here for the first time.

Apart from that, you will find a bran tub of occasional verse, whimsical musings and a smattering of more serious poems and lyrics.

Acknowledgements

As far as the present volume is concerned, first and definitely foremost among those I must thank are my friends Philip and Julie Porter of Porter Press. Without their enthusiasm and determination, you would not be reading this. I am immensely grateful to them and their team, not least among whom is the designer and illustrator Martin Port who has done such a brilliant job bringing these pages to life.

To have a Foreword contributed by one of today's foremost lyricists is a rare privilege. Tim Rice's unique gifts as a wordsmith have graced the worlds of theatre and film for over half a century. Many of his songs are now simply part of the fabric, to live on in our hearts for all time. I thank him sincerely.

I should also like to salute several people who have performed or championed these verses over the years: the celebrated two-piano team of Richard Markham and David Nettle, who commissioned the *Carnival* verses; the late Willie Rushton, who recorded them for Yorkshire TV back in 1987; the distinguished pianist Roger Vignoles and mezzo-soprano Sarah Walker, and the renowned Canadian virtuoso Marc André Hamelin and soprano Jody Karin Appelbaum – two duos who have recorded selections of my songs; and Cantabile (The London Quartet) who have had some in their repertoire for over three decades.

As well as expressing my gratitude to all those mentioned above, there are four people, sadly no longer with us, who encouraged me along the way: Andrew Best (literary agent), Michael Ember (radio producer), Sue Hill (publisher) and, as mentioned above, Peter Skellern (singer, songwriter and priest). I owe them much, as I do my beloved parents – and their arbitrary collection of gramophone recordings.

I also thank the dedicatee of this book, my wife Jillie, for her constant support and sagacity. She has been the first person to hear or read almost everything in this volume. I have greatly benefitted from her advice and criticism. Last but not least, *chapeau* to my lifelong friend J N Woolcock who has taken up the (unpaid) role of assistant editor, offering many useful comments, amendments and suggestions. I have been persuaded by him to keep some of these in the text, sometimes against my better judgement.

Jeremy Nicholas
Great Bardfield, February 2022

Carnival of the Animals

To accompany *La Grande Fantaisie Zoologique* by Camille Saint-Saëns

These verses were commissioned by the piano duo team of David Nettle and Richard Markham. The *Carnival of the Animals* is the great composer off duty, a *jeu d'esprit* intended for the entertainment of his friends by a man who had a surprising reputation as a practical joker. Ironically, he banned publication of the entire work (apart from its most famous section, 'The Swan') until after his death fearing that such high-jinks would damage his reputation as a serious composer.

The work's 14 short movements – arguably Saint-Saëns's most famous and frequently-played piece – were finally given their first public performance on 25 February 1922… without a narrator in sight. The tradition of interspersing the music with comic verses began thanks to Goddard Lieberson of Columbia Records and conductor Andre Kostelanetz in 1949. Ogden Nash, then at the height of his fame as America's best-known purveyor of humorous verse, was asked to provide something on each section for a new recording; Noël Coward was booked as speaker.

It is Nash's verses that have become indelibly associated with the music. Personally, I think they should be retired without a pension and sent to the nearest recycling plant. As someone who has narrated many orchestra/speaker works and been lumbered with the Nash verses more than once, modern audiences (in the UK at least) find the many dated references in the verses simply baffling. So it was with a feeling of immense relief and gratitude that I was able to write and perform my own attempt (joining those of several others over the years) to replace Nash.

They were first heard in October 1985 as part of a Saint-Saëns 150th birthday concert mounted by Nettle and Markham in the Queen Elizabeth Hall, London, Since then, they have accompanied performances of *Carnival of the Animals* with full orchestra, with the original chamber ensemble score, in an arrangement for two pianos (and recorder!) and even for organ. The chamber version recorded for BBC Radio 2 (Nettle and Markham as the pianists) was subsequently released as a CD in 2006. The verses were revised in 2014.

ORDER OF PROCESSION

1 Introduction and Royal March of the Lion

2 Hens and Cocks ... Wild Asses

3 The Tortoises ... The Elephant

4 The Kangaroo ... The Aquarium

5 Persons with long ears

6 The Cuckoo in the heart of the woods

7 The Aviary

8 Pianists ... Fossils

9 The Swan

10 Finale

Music cues: 𝄞 ♪♪♩

INTRODUCTION and ROYAL MARCH OF THE LION

In a suburb of Paris, some years ago now,

Was a highly unusual Zoo.

It was privately owned by a Monsieur Saint-Saëns.

The price of admission? Cent sous.

Now Saint-Saëns, you must know, was a famous musician –

The *crème de la crème* in his day –

But all he's remembered for now are his animals.

Oh – he was French, by the way.

He started with **tortoises**, then a few **chickens**

And other conventional pets;

They would sit in the study while Saint-Saëns was writing

Concertos and piano quintets.

Two highly-appreciative musical **goldfish**

Then came to reside in the house,

And a singing **canary** whose trick was to warble

The Blue Danube Waltz (by J. Strauss).

This eccentric but pleasant domestic arrangement
Rapidly got out of hand.
When Saint-Saëns brought an **African elephant** back
He could see it was time to expand.
This odd little man (who was known, apropos,
To all of his friends as 'Camille'),
Decided to keep his menagerie housed
In a replica of the Bastille.
It was built in the garden of Chateau Saint-Saëns
At the bottom of which was a lake;
And the animals ate only *filet de boeuf*
(Which translated means "best fillet steak").
They were fed by two keepers that Saint-Saëns employed –
Two young **pianists** whom he had met.
In return for their keep they looked after the Zoo
And played non-stop Saint-Saëns in duet.
Now on one special day (and the same day each year)
Saint-Saëns let the animals free.
To the music he'd written especially for them
They marched through the streets of Paris.
The procession was led by an elderly **lion**
Who admitted himself that his roar
Was more like a cough, but they let him lead off
Because everyone else knew the score.
He was no longer rampant, but still, like a king,
Held his head high with pride, lion-hearted.
With a look of disdain, he roared, shook his mane
And with that, Saint-Saëns's Carnival started.

HENS AND COCKS ... WILD ASSES

The next to emerge through the front garden gate,
As the lion went slowly ahead,
Were a paltry assortment of chickens and hens
Plus two cocks and a Rhode Island Red.
The neighbours who lived either side of Saint-Saëns
Thought the pageant decidedly strange.
As they spied through the gap in their curtains they said,
"Now we know what he meant by 'free range'.
We don't mind the cockerel each morning at five
But it's really too much of a strain
To listen to all of that music each day –
And the same piece *again* and *again*."
At that moment, two asses who came from Tibet
Galloped out at a frightening speed.
One was a donkey and one was a mule –
Which was which they had never agreed.
"It's a wonderful treat," said one ass to the other,
"To listen to Saint-Saëns quite free."
Said his friend, "Yes, I know and it all goes to show
Just what asses your neighbours can be!"

THE TORTOISES AND THE ELEPHANT

Saint-Saëns's Carnival moved at a leisurely pace
Because next in this grand Noah's Ark
Were two tortoises nicknamed Johann and Sebastian –
Gifts from his friend Offenbach.

* * *

The dignified elephant carried Saint-Saëns.
"What an honour!" he said. "I'm so proud."
Then, forgetting himself, all at once started dancing
And waving his trunk at the crowd!

THE KANGAROO … THE AQUARIUM

The Parisians clapped the parade as it wound
Its circuitous route through the city.
Flags of red, white and blue! Shouts of "*Vive le Zoo!*"
Oh, the whole thing looked frightfully pretty.
The children yelled, "Look at the lion and elephant!
Look at that sweet kangaroo!"
With one bound it leapt over the head of the lion
Who roared, "Oi! Get back in the queue!"
The kangaroo paid not the slightest attention
But rushed off in front at great speed.
It had reached Notre Dame when a friendly gendarme said,
"That's it! That's enough! Where's his lead?"
The Saint-Saëns aquarium followed behind,
For the fish couldn't walk, that was plain.
He'd suggested they swam down the river one year
But the fish had said that was insane.
They elected to stay in the fish tank instead –
The decision was put to the vote –
So the elephant said he would pull it along
And it travelled, of course, on a float.

PERSONS WITH LONG EARS

On the steps of the Opéra everyone paused
To acknowledge the orchestra's cheers.
Making notes on the pageant were two music Critics –
Two persons with very long ears.
They scoffed and they scowled with a sceptical scorn
As they scribbled their scurrilous scrawl.
But despite what they wrote and the way that they spoke
No-one took any notice at all.

THE CUCKOO IN THE HEART OF THE WOODS

All this excitement was tiring for some,
So the elephant called for a break
By using his trunk – a trunk call, you see – [1]
And Saint-Saëns said, "Let them eat cake."

So the Carnaval stopped in the Bois de Boulogne
Where they all had a drink and a munch.
The lion said, "This is all right for a snack
But I'd like a whole horse for my lunch."

They were just moving off when, some distance away,
They heard in the wood a bird sing.
The kangaroo sprang to attention on hearing
The very first cuckoo in Spring.

[1] I doubt if younger readers will understand this (Ed.) Too bad (JN)

𝄞 ♫♩

THE AVIARY

But what had become of the feathered inhabitants
Saint-Saëns had tamed for his zoo?
All at once, everybody looked up at the rooftops
As birdsong broke out – right on cue!

𝄞 ♫♩

A chorus of blackbirds and thrushes and larks
From the wings of the Opéra was heard,
And one of the persons with very long ears said,
"Well, who'd have believed it? My word!"
"It's a beautiful sound," said his friend, "and a pity
The management couldn't arrange
To engage some of *these* at exorbitant fees
And hire something in tune for a change!"
The canary (who warbled *The Blue Danube Waltz*)
Led the choir in a joyful re-tweet
As a small Budgerigar flew off down the boulevard
To deposit a *carte de visite*.

* * *

PIANISTS AND FOSSILS

Behind the aquarium an upright piano
Positioned on top of a dray
Was pulled through the streets by an eighteen-hand horse –
What a shame that the Horse couldn't play!
For the zoo-keeper/pianists Saint-Saëns employed,
(This is something I should have explained),
Were still on Grade Three and so, unlike the animals,
Hadn't been quite fully trained.

* * *

Incidentally, tied to the side of the upright
(A custom peculiar to France)
The traditional skeleton bounced up and down
In a grimly macabre sort of dance.
This fossilised person was highly mysterious –
Everyone there asked "Who was it?"
A wit in the crowd said, "I think it's the skeleton
Saint-Saëns has got in the closet!"

THE SWAN

Placidly waddling along at the rear
And causing a huge traffic jam
Was the swan from the lake Saint-Saëns had in his garden –
Yes, that was where Saint-Saëns' swan swam.

FINALE

The Carnival stopped at the Place de la Concorde
And there in the midst of the City
It was met by the President of the Republic,
His wife and a six-man committee.
"*Bonjour*, Monsieur Saint-Saëns," the President said.
"Merci beaucoup for all you have done.
Many thanks for your zoo and the carnival too
And for making good music such fun!"
The elderly lion gave a roar of approval
And everyone else gave a cheer,
Saint-Saëns took a bow and they all made a vow
To be back at the same time next year!

The End

A Throne of Your Own

THE DANISH LOT

CANUTE
b.995? cr.1016 d.1035

Of Danish birth was King Canute –
A vicious Scandinavian brute
Whose hobby was to rob and loot
And generally persecute.
The Brits. did not want a dispute
(Their army was, alas, minute).
The Vikings, though, were resolute
And anyone they met en route
They'd either capture and recruit
Or summarily execute.
The King, according to repute,
Was both politically acute –
Incontrovertibly astute –
And altogether rather cute,
Yet had one fatal attribute:
He thought his rule was absolute.
So one day, off the Isle of Bute,
While swimming in his birthday suit,
He told the waves to revolute!
The ocean didn't give a hoot
And nearly drowned the silly coot.
He swam ashore in disrepute
(The Danish lords in hot pursuit)
And no-one bothered to salute.

"The King's become irresolute,
A fact," they said, "we can't refute.
Let's vote to give Canute the boot."
They locked him in an institute
And had to find a substitute.
Thus ends the reign of King Canute.

HAROLD 1 (Harefoot)
b.1017 cr.1035 d.1040
and
HARDICANUTE
b.1018 cr.1040 d.1042

Canute was succeeded by Harold (Part One)
But I can't tell you anything more.
He just sort of reigned and then just sort of died
And was frankly a bit of a bore.

His brother named Hardicanute took his place
And the English said, "Something must be
Quite rotten in Denmark's condition if *this*
Is the top of its family tree.
If you *must* come and rule us, send someone exciting!" –
They looked on this Dane with disdain –
"Send us Hamlet or Hans Christian Andersen, *please!*,
Not another unmemorable reign."

* * *

THE SAXON LOT

EDWARD THE CONFESSOR
b.1004? cr.1042 d.1066

Edward the Confessor's rather famous,
Though for reasons that are not entirely clear.
He built Westminster Abbey for the English Tourist Board
But in point of fact was very rarely here.
At confessions I am sure he was a winner,
And he founded an historic abbey church,
But King Edward as a king was a disaster
According to historical research.

* * *

HAROLD II (Godwinson)
b.1022 cr.1066 d.1066

The last Saxon king had a very brief reign –
He had just been crowned Harold (Part Two)
When a message arrived. It said 'NORMANS INVADING' [2]
And everyone asked, "Norman who?"
Duke William it was who'd set sail with some friends
On a day trip to England from France.
He'd declared he was going to conquer the Brits.
But his friends murmured, "Blimey, some chance!"
At Hastings he led them through Passport Control
And things went quite swimmingly till
King Harold arrived and confronted the Duke
And said, "Halt! What's your name?" He said, "Bill."
"Well look, Bill", said Harold, "this sort of behaviour
Is something we English deplore.
Now get back to Normandy!" "No!" said the Duke.
"Right", said Harold. "That's it, chum. It's war!"
The Normans lined up on the beach while the English
Came down like a wolf on the fold,
But their cohorts were rusty and covered in mud
And the seafront was *terribly* cold.
They threw in the towel in the end, I'm afraid –
To the Normans they had to defer.
(The towel, as you know, was picked up and dried out
And is still on display in Bayeux.)

[2] Is there an apostrophe missing in 'Normans invading'? (Ed.)

No (JN)

For the Normans, the day out had been a success;
For the Brits., it was one in the eye.
(The same could be said of King Harold as well
When an arrow went slightly awry.)
And that was the end of the Battle of Hastings,
The last time, I'm glad to relate,
That Britain was ever successfully conquered
And 1066 was the date.

THE NORMAN LOT

WILLIAM I (The Conqueror)
b.1027 cr.1066 d.1087

William the Conqueror marched up to London
To crown himself William (Part One).
The Normans, of course, were delighted at this,
But the English said, "Lads, we've been done.
He can't speak the language, he's not one of us
And nobody asked him to come."
But they had to admit that the fellow had style
And had got them all under his thumb.
He took all the Englishmen's lands and estates.
"What a gaul!" they all said. "What a crook!"
He invented the curfew, the Tower of London
And published the famed Domesday Book.
He imported French polish, French wine and French beans
French onions, French fries and French bread.
He'd have brought in French horns and French windows as well
But by that time King William was dead.

WILLIAM II (William Rufus)
b.1056? cr.1087 d.1100

Rufus the Red Head reigned here [3]
He would shout and scream and swear.
He had a frightful temper
Just because he had red hair.
Barons and Lords all pondered.
"We didn't mind his father, but
William, he takes the biscuit.
What a horrid ginger nut."
Then one lovely summer's day
While hunting in the wood,
Someone shot him by mistake
And the Lords all shouted: "Good!"
Goodbye to silly Billy!
No-one was the least downcast.
Rufus the Red Head reigned here –
Carrot Top had gone at last.

* * *

[3] Can be sung to the tune of Rudolph the Red-nose Reindeer (JN.)

Does this really work as a concept? (Ed)

HENRY I
b.1068 cr.1100 d.1135

King Henry (Part One), who was next on the throne,
Turned out to be not at all bad.
Born in England, you see, he would logically be
Better off than his brother or Dad.
He was firm, he was strict, he was cunning, but fair
And, to further and strengthen his cause,
This practical King did the sensible thing
By acquiring some Scottish in-laws.
He and Matilda (the name of his wife)
Were happy as happy could be.
To add to their joy, she gave birth to a boy
Who should have been William (Part Three).
But the lad went out sailing one dark, stormy night:
In the Channel, the boat ran aground.
A pity for him as he'd not learned to swim
And, of course, ended up getting drowned.
As Henry lay dying, the Lords gathered round
And said : "Sire, you're the best Norman yet.
We're all quite agreed that your daughter succeed,
As she's married to a Plantagenet.
Furthermore, when you're gone, all us English are going
To call you King Henry Beauclerc.
"You're a scholar," they said, "you can write, you're well read,
But above all you've not got red hair."

STEPHEN
b.1097 cr.1135 & 1141 d.1154
and
MATILDA
b.1102 cr.1141 d.1154

Having met King Henry's daughter (Queen Matilda),
The Barons had emphatic second thoughts.
"She's a woman and she's spiteful.
Let's crown Stephen, who's just frightful.
They can fight it out between them in the courts."

Now this Stephen was a nephew of King Henry –
Another jumped-up Norman blighter who
Was *way* down the official list for ruling
(But then foreigners have never learnt to queue).

Whatever was our noble country coming to
When a man called Stephen's asked to come and reign?
You can't have kings called *Stephen* ruling England!
Whatever next? King Gary or King Wayne?

Once he'd got the crown, 'King Steve' proved so pathetic
That the Barons lost their patience in the end.
"For God's sake, where's Matilda?
Look, if someone hasn't killed her
Bring her over on the ferry from Ostend."

They found King Henry's daughter (Queen Matilda)
And England's rightful heir was thus restored.
But the Barons, to be candid,
Weren't quite sure, for when she landed
Queen Matilda said she'd changed her name to Maud.

Matilda / Maud gave Stephen's lot a thrashing
To establish that she really was the Queen.
It came as quite a shock
To find this fella in a frock
Was ten times worse than even Steve had been.
The Barons looked agog at one another.
"Oh well," they said. "We've been and done it now.
She might be England's rightful,
But, by George, she's not just spiteful,
She's a domineering, avaricious cow.

I think we'd better go and have a ponder."
So the Barons (with the Clergy) ummed and urred
And agreed to bring back Stephen from retirement,
Though they *still* weren't certain which one they preferred!

After Maud, the English had a referendum
Not to have a Queen again for years and years.
Moreover, after Steve and Maud
There were no more Normans left (thank Gawd!)
And the English gave three very hearty cheers.

* * *

THE PLANTAGENET LOT

HENRY II (Curtmantel)
b.1133 cr.1154 d.1189

The second King Henry to sit on the throne
Was the second King William's double:
As he too had red hair and came over from France
You could tell there was bound to be trouble.

He began rather well by uniting the land
And was brim full of novel ideas;
For example, a system called 'scutage' which lasted [4]
For hundreds and hundreds of years.

He brought in the Jury that still sits in court
To decide if you're guilty or not.
(Up till then, you were innocent if you'd survived
Being hung, drawn and quartered, then shot.)

His best friend was Chancellor Thomas à Becket
And, finding one day they were skint,
They decided to open a sweet shop together
And called it Ye Olde Royal Mint.

[4] What exactly is scutage? (Ed.)

Haven't got a clue (JN)

They made so much money that Henry said, "Tom,
The Church here is going to pot.
The Bishops and Clergy aren't towing the line,
So I'm making you head of the lot."
Tom flatly refused, but King Henry insisted:
"À Beckett, a bishop you'll be!"
And that was the end of a beautiful friendship
For neither could ever agree.

Archbishop à Beckett and Henry fell out
And all meaningful dialogue ceased,
Till at last, in a temper, King Henry yelled, "Someone!
Get rid of that so-and-so priest!"

He shouldn't have said it, he realised that,
For straightaway two noble Lords
Found Thomas à Beckett inside his cathedral
And stabbed him to death with their swords.

The King was so sorry, he put up a shrine
(Pilgrims *still* come from near and from far)
And walked barefoot from London to pay his respects.
(It was quicker than going by car).

Then everyone turned against Henry the Second –
His children and even his wife.
Soon after, defeated, defied and defamed,
King Henry took leave of this life.

Moral:
The one thing that monarchs should not *ever* do
(How often has this to be said?)
Is to make their best friend an Archbishop, because
It will all end in tears before bed.

* * *

RICHARD I (Lionheart)
b.1157 cr.1189 d.1199

The monarch who rules over us
Must be an Anglophile.
The best ones stand on balconies,
Shake hands a lot and smile.

The monarch who despises
All his subjects as a rule
Is, at the most, an arrant knave
And, at the least, a fool.

King Richard was the latter sort
And known as Coeur de Lion –
A fact that all historians
Of any note agree on.

Exceptionally strong and brave
And thick as two short planks,
King Dick lived here for just six months.
He reigned ten years! Gee, thanks.

The Brits. thought he was Superman,
Clint Eastwood, God, the works,
As Dick and his Crusaders
Fought the Infidels – the Turks.

But like every English Test Match
When we drop a catch that's vital,
Like an English tennis player
Who will *never* win the title,

So King Richard fought Aladdin [5]
In the heathen Holy Land.
If he'd only stuck to grass courts
And not tried to play on sand!

The English army stuck it out
In tents (as was the heat), [6]
But in 1192
Admitted its defeat.

Yet, though he lost the final set,
King Richard homeward came
To accept that customary prize
For English losers – Fame.

But soon he left to fight in France
And someone killed him there.
Well, as the French so aptly put it:
"Tough, *mais c'est la guerre*".

* * *

[5] Don't you mean Saladin? (Ed.) Who's Saladin? (JN)
[6] The heat was in tents? (Ed.) Yes (JN)

JOHN
b.1167 cr.1199 d.1216

Bad King John is on the throne
(Whimper, whine and mutter)
Worst King that we've ever known
(Is the bloke a nutter?)
He's King Richard's youngest brother
(Grumble, grouse and groan)
Please, sir, can we have another?
(Mumble, mope and moan)

Terror, bloodshed, pillage, rape
(Misery and woe)
From King John there's no escape
(Will he ever go?)

Can't he spend his reign abroad?
(Discontent and doom)
The Amazon's still unexplored
(Bellyache and gloom)

The Barons, too, have had enough
(Snivel, weep and wail)
With bad King John they're getting tough
(Tremble, quake and quail)

Negotiations there have been
(About time too! At last!)
The two sides meet! It's 1215.
(The clock says twenty-past)

In a field at Runnymede
(Whinny, moo-moo, baa)
Magna Carta's been agreed
(Blah-blah-blah-blah-blah)

Bad King John's cut down to size
(Yah-boo, sucks and jeers)
Hope the evil blighter dies
(Crocodile tears).

The King of Instruments

Back in 1992, the distinguished organist Thomas Trotter asked me to narrate a piece for the unusual combination of organ and narrator to be performed in Birmingham Town Hall. It was by the American composer William Albright. Its aim was to show off, in an entertaining and accessible manner, the King of Instruments with short examples of Albright's own music, demonstrating the various sections of the organ, interspersed with some verses of his own.

Two years later, Thomas suggested we repeat the piece. I demurred on the grounds that although Albright's music was all right, his verses were terrible. I volunteered to write replacements – and the results were first performed in a lunchtime concert (from Birmingham Town Hall again) broadcast on BBC Radio 3. Albright's publisher was not pleased, so in 2012 I revised my verses so that they could be performed without any reference to Albright.

Organists can now make their own selection of any appropriate non-copyright organ works to use with these verses.

1 INTRODUCTION

The mighty King of Instruments
Before us stands arrayed!
Half innocent, half monster,
It beckons to be played.
Four keyboards? Surely one's enough –
And for the feet one more!
With rows and rows of gaudy pipes –
Whatever are they for?
With buttons, switches, levers, knobs
The console fairly bristles.
Intimidating? Not at all –
It's just a box with whistles.
But how can music be brought forth
From such a savage beast?
And who aspires to play the thing?
An octopus, at least!
The mammoth slumbers, breathing yet,
A Byzantine antique.
The stops are drawn, the organ wakes,
Now let us hear it speak.

2 THE MANUALS

The piano has a keyboard;
The organ has as well –
Except we call them manuals
And this one's called the Swell.

The sound can swell from soft to loud
And make the floor vibrate.
But to aggravate the neighbours
Use this manual called the Great.

The party wall is shaking
So we turn with some relief
To the dulcet sounds of manual three –
The Choir or Positif.

[The Solo is the topmost one.
Don't use it, I beseech
Unless your arms are very long –
It's rather hard to reach!][7]

---

[7] If the organ has not got a Solo manual, omit these four lines.

3 THE PEDALS

The pedals sound the lowest notes
Or what we call 'the bass'.
How envied the executant
Who plays with polished grace
This wooden keyboard out of view.
How easily he floats!
How come he cannot see his shoes
And yet hits all the notes?
How many village organists
Have stumbled in this dance?
How many simply shut their eyes
Then pray and take a chance?
The organist performs his steps
While sitting on his seat.
To play a tune with heel and toe
Is surely quite a feat.

4 THE FLUES

The orchestra has different sections.
Each one has a name –
The Woodwind, Brass, et cetera;
The organ is the same.
The basic sounds are Flues and Reeds,
That's all you need to know.
We'll take you through them one by one
(Or is it blow by blow?).
Some organs have these push-pull stops
While others have small switches.
They've all got different labels
To remind you just what which is.
The Flue called 'Diapason'
Every organ built possesses.
You can hear just what it sounds like
When the keyboard he depresses.

5 THE REEDS

There's a section of the organ
That we haven't heard as yet
Which is made of stops like Trumpet,
Horn, Cornopean, Clarinet.
There's the Tromba and the Posaune
And there's nothing that succeeds
Quite like pulling all the stops out
For a blast upon the Reeds.

6 THE MIXTURES

Every single key that's pressed down
Has a corresponding pipe...
One pipe per note per stop, I thought,
But that's a load of tripe.
For next you'll hear the Mixture stops;
Each key sounds two or three
Quite separate notes which sound as one
Simultaneously.
Who was it who invented this?
I neither know nor care.
It proves the rule that pipe dreams
Are nothing but thin air.

7 **THE MUTATIONS**

You've heard the Diapason pipes.
You've heard the Pedals, too.
You've heard the Mixtures, Reeds and Flues –
Well, here is something new.
There's the Larigot and Nazard
There's the Tierce, the Quint and Quarte
Which play at different pitches
To the one you would have thought.
They're what are called Mutation stops –
It's very complicated.
I think I'll stop and ask my friend
If he will demonstrate it.

8 **THE FLUTE**

The flute is next. I love it so.
More pleasing than the piccolo,
More flighty than the clarinet
More racey than the oboe, yet
To play the flute is something I
Would never personally try.
With hands held thus I should have thought
That just to keep it up you ought
To have some kind of arm support.
The flute, I rather think you'll find,
Was almost certainly designed

By someone who had won a bet
To see if, for a laugh, he'd get
Some simple soul to stand like this
And blow into its orifice.
Far easier, when all is said,
To play the keyboard flute instead.

9 THE TUBA

The organ has a repertoire
That's long as it is broad
And roughly ninety-five per cent
Is totally ignored.
There are symphonies, concertos,
Fantasias, fugues, sonatas,
Choral preludes by the cart-load,
Simply tumbrils of toccatas,
Variations and transcriptions
All of which are quite entrancing.
In fact, its only limits are
For Scottish country dancing.
And so, to prove the point now,
The Tuba struts its stuff –
And unlike its brass band counterpart,
It won't run out of puff.

10 THE VOIX CELESTE

Of all the stops I love the best
The hazy, shimm'ring Voix Celeste
Is one I frequently request.
Perhaps you never would have guessed
That someone who's so prone to jest
And looks so calm and self-possessed
Occasionally feels stressed.
Well, I'm exactly like the rest.
So there you have it. I've confessed.
If you're the same, may I suggest
To get your troubles off your chest
Just take it easy, have a rest
And close your eyes with the Celeste.

11 THE ORGANIST

The stuntman and the acrobat
Are people we admire
And that man who crossed Niagara Falls
By walking on a wire,
Lion tamers with their lions
Locked inside their cages –
Yet an organist pulls stops, plays keys
And also turns the pages.

They're conjurers whose sleights of hand
Defy the ears and eyes
In a self-contained gymnasium
On which they exercise.
Up and down the organ bench
They slide from cheek to cheek;
They get through two new pairs of trousers
Almost every week.
Upon their feet are leather thongs
Which once, perhaps, were shoes.
Yet somehow from this mayhem
There pours forth their wondrous muse.
So let the organ thunder,
And the Diapasons sing.
Let it rage and roar and sigh and soar –
The organ is the king.

Raspberries and Other Trifles

Tales for Discerning Delinquents

The author takes a modest pride
In offering this handy guide
For children who suspect they may
Be turning both their parents grey –
Delinquents who perhaps don't know
Exactly how far they can go.
It's aim by illustrated verse
To tempt them into doing worse.
For this, the volume is, you'll find,
The *ne plus ultra* of its kind.
Each portrait and each tale are FACT,
Though, since I am a man of tact,
The characters have been disguised
In case they might be recognised.
More pertinently, three or four
On reading this might go to law:
Incorrigible rascals who,
If publicly exposed, would sue.
But never mind. I guaranteed
You'll know at least one personally.

GAVIN CLINCH

Whose life ended fruitlessly

Of all the children I have met
The most undisciplined as yet
Was Gavin Clinch, a child of six
Who got up to all sorts of tricks.
His parents thought the world of him;
In my view this was rather dim.
They let him do just as he pleased –
He yelled,
He spat,
He burped,
He sneezed,
And
Didn't show the least concern –
Ah well, some parents never learn.
For (while I don't agree with caning)
Strict, relentless toilet-training
Coupled with a daily clout
Would soon have sorted Gavin out.
The folly of their lax approach
Was shown when all three went by coach
To London for the Lord Mayor's show.
Our Gavin did not want to go.
He yelled, he spat, et cetera,
Abused the driver and Papa,

And put his mother in a flap
By being sick near Watford Gap.
Arrived in London – what a fuss! –
They had to drag him off the bus.
Then travelled on the Underground
To Blackfriars Bridge where soon they found
A most convenient place to spy
The Grand Procession passing by.
His parents cheered and clapped and waved
But, oh dear, Gavin misbehaved
(No need to spell out how or what…)
Suffice to say they left the spot
And hurried to within the walls
Of Wren's magnificent St Paul's.
They thought their offspring ought to see
This shrine of English history
Where Wellington and others rest,
But Gavin Clinch was not impressed.
He ran off down the centre aisle –
His parents lost him for a while –
Then all at once they heard a sound
Which echoed round and round and round.
The Clinches were amazed to see
Up in the Whispering Gallery
Their son! And Gavin (oh, the shame!)
Was blowing raspberries for a game:

Not one,

Not two,

Not three

or four

But eighteen, nineteen

Now a score.

It sounded very, very rude,

Quite out of keeping with the mood….

More like a liner leaving dock.

A group of nuns collapsed in shock,

While others tolerantly smiled,

"My *goodness*, what a noisy child!"

The scores of tourists gathered there

(And one or two had knelt in prayer)

Tut-tutted as they looked aghast

And winced at each successive blast.

The verger wished the organist

Would make an effort to resist

Such modern works, so harsh and stark:

"Why can't he stick to dear old Bach

And play this awful stuff at home?"

As raspberries echoed round the dome.

The Dean, who heard them from the crypt,

Rushed up the stairs red-faced, tight-lipped,

Suppressing thoughts at every stride

Of imminent infanticide.

He spotted Gavin standing there,

Crept up behind him, grabbed his hair,

Frogmarched him down into the nave,
And cried, "How dare you misbehave!
I'll knock you into kingdom come."
Then spanked him soundly on the bum.
The Clinches rushed up in alarm.
The Dean held Gavin by the arm.
"Is this your child?"
"He is," they said.
"And please don't cuff him round the head.
It's just high spirits, Mr Dean,"
Who mumbled something quite obscene
And spluttered, "Blowing raspberries here
Disturbs the sacred atmosphere.
This boy is a complete disgrace."
Then Gavin blew one in his face,
And ran straight out across the road,
Oblivious of the Highway Code.
He didn't look to left or right,
And – oh! It was a dreadful sight –
A ten-ton juggernaut from Dover
Couldn't stop and ran him over.
The Clinches thought it rotten luck
To have their son squashed by a truck.
The Dean consoled them. "Have you thought
That God became quite over-wrought
And *had* to put his foot down here?"
"The driver did just that, I fear,"
Said Mr Clinch, who thought it odd
That juggernauts were Acts of God.

MARY-JANE and EMILY

Whose viewing habits came unstuck

I wonder if you've been to tea
With Mary-Jane and Emily,
Twin sisters both with golden curls,
The prettiest of little girls?
They're similar in many ways –
Not least in how their tempers blaze.
At tea-time, far from eating food,
The twins are resolutely glued
To television, when they fight
For what they're going to watch that night.
They never ever can agree
Upon which programme they will see.
They pull each other's hair about
And scratch and kick and sulk and pout.
Then one day, Emily let fly –
She hit her sister in the eye
Because she wanted Tom and Jerry.
Gracious! Her vocabulary!
Mary-Jane picked up the jelly,
Missed her sister, hit the telly.
SPLAT! It landed on the screen.
(A pity. It was tangerine.)
Unfortunately, some of it
Ran down inside a tiny slit

And there coagulated, which
Jammed up the programme-channel switch
The telly stayed forever more
Immovably on Channel Four.
The sisters went to see their Mum.
"Please ask the engineer to come!"
He came, he saw, and then declared,
"This telly cannot be repaired,
A model that was not designed
For jelly fights of any kind.
There's nothing for it, tell your mother,
But to go and buy another."
There and then, without delay,
He took the wretched thing away.
Oh, the wailing! Oh, the tears!
Oh, the sodden little dears!
Poor Emily and Mary-Jane
Have never had a fight again.
They have to talk and read instead,
And go much earlier to bed.

* * *

The moral here is plain to see
Don't watch the box while having tea.

AMANDA PUGH

Who became fat and famous

The least attractive child I knew
Was certainly Amanda Pugh.
One couldn't help observing that
She was, to put it bluntly, fat.
(Before the feminists complain,
By this I don't mean she was plain
Or ugly in the slightest way.)
Her temperament was bright and gay,
Outgoing, jolly, rarely sad,
And both her parents said she had
A captivating smile (but which
In fact disguised a nervous twitch).
Now, while it's true that there are lots
Of pre-pubescent girls with spots,
And, even from the middle classes,
Some who wear corrective glasses;
And while everybody understands
When something's wrong with someone's glands,
Amanda, cursed with all of these,
Succumbed to yet one more disease:
She over-ate. She stuffed it in!
Her tummy was a refuse bin.
Her primary delight in life
Was sitting with a fork and knife
And eating everything in sight.
She hardly ever paused to bite –

Her mouth was like a small machine
That ploughed through Mrs Pugh's cuisine:
Chocolates, puddings, jellies, sweets,
Lamb cutlets and all kinds of meats,
Meringues, éclairs and marzipan,
Potatoes, dumplings, strawberry flan,
Nougat, doughnuts, *pounds* of butter,
(Sometimes her Papa would mutter,
As she crammed in more lasagne
"Blimey 'Riley, girl, how can yer?")
Guzzling baked beans, veg and fish
With double portions of each dish.
And after all this she'd implore,
"I'm hungry, Mummy! Give me MORE!"
When she'd remembered to say, "Please",
She'd tuck into the Stilton cheese,
The Cheddar, Brie and Camembert
And then attack the dining-chair.
(Amanda used to like to savour
Bits of wood. She loved the flavour.)
At nine o'clock she'd go to bed
But first she'd eat a loaf of bread
And just a little more rice pud.
I've not met anyone who could
Dispose of so much food per day –
Not even an adult gourmet.
So by the time that she was eight
She was distinctly overweight;

To be exact, she was colossal.
A dropsical rhinoceros'll
Gives you roughly the idea –
A sort of squishy-squashy sphere.
The word they use is 'adipose';
To me, there's only one word: GROSS.
Eventually Amanda Pugh
Left school and wondered what to do.
"I know," she thought, "I'll go and slim."
But once she'd squeezed into the gym
The people there said, "Sorry. No.
We can't reduce the status quo.
The fact is, sweetheart, you are fat.
You'll have to learn to live with that."
Amanda did not give up hope:
She seized hold of a long wire rope
Which had attached a heavy weight…
Now was this luck? Or was it Fate?
For shortly afterwards she moved
(And both her Mum and Dad approved)
To Russia, where she changed her name
And has achieved a sort of fame.
When watching an athletics match
There's one sight you are bound to catch:
Amanda Pugh, who used to be
A byword for obesity.
She's now Amanda Pughsilowa
'Peoples' Champion Hammer Thrower'.

DOMINIC FORMAL de HYDE

Who addressed himself to men's rights

Young Dominic Formal de Hyde
Was half French (on his father's side).
Like many youthful extroverts
He loved to look up ladies' skirts.
This phase is one that every boy
Appears to go through and enjoy.
Though one, I think it's fair to say,
Most people wish would go away.
For, on the whole, it disenchants
One's mother's friends and maiden aunts,
Who do not like their underwear
Subjected to a small boy's stare.
But when the time came to submerge
This normal adolescent urge,
Dominic Formal de Hyde did
Something I should call 'misguided':
He asked his mother "Would you buy,
A summer frock for me to try?"
His mother kindly acquiesced,
And soon our Dominic was dressed
Up in an elegant chemise
That came down just below his knees.
The cut was flattering and chic,
The garment suited his physique.
His father said he liked the dress,
Une réponse a l'emporté-pièce! [8]

[8] You can't translate it, I can tell
    I had to look it up as well.

"Mon Dieu, the boy is in his teens,
Why can't he wear a shirt and jeans?
Mon fils sers une vraie risée."
Or, as an Englishman would say,
"My son will be a laughing stock".
(His father came from Languedoc.)
But Dominic ignored his scorn:
"I don't see why when girls have worn
Men's trousers, jackets, ties and shirts."
His Dad conceded that this view
Was, most unfortunately, true.
In fact, it was beyond dispute:
His daughter wore a pin-stripe suit.
Soon afterwards Formal de Hyde
Passed three A-levels and applied
To Oxford University
To read, yes, sociology.
His first day up, when he appeared
In floral dress, stout shoes and beard
Caused several students to demur,
"Is she a him? Is he a her?"
They thought it an enormous joke
To see an ordinary bloke
In such a strange mode of attire.
One wag suggested they inquire
If Dominic was on the pill.
"My God this place has gone downhill,"
The Chancellor was heard to say.
"You couldn't do this in *my* day."

A meeting of the Dons was called,
Who said, "Well frankly, we're appalled.
It really is beyond the bounds
To wear these off-the-shoulder gowns.
Fetch the blighter here and tell him
No more skirts or we'll expel him."
So Dominic arrived to face
The learned Dons and state his case.
(He wore a frock of deep maroon
That he had bought that afternoon –
A lucky bargain off the peg
Revealing just a hint of leg.)
The Dean was openly impressed
And told the Chaplain, who confessed
Maroon was very much his taste.
"If I were thinner round the waist
I'd buy a purple frock today –
Whatever would the Bishop say?"
The Chancellor said, "Listen, lad!
We do not like the way you're clad.
Now, either wear your college gown
Or we shall have to send you down."
"I fail to see," cried Dominic
"Why you should think I am unique.
To wear a dress is nothing new
In Greece, in Fiji or Peru.
In Scotland it is not a crime –
An Arab wears one all the time.

And furthermore it's pretty clear
That you let lots of people here
Wear frocks and skirts, twin-sets and pearls..."
"Yes Dominic, we call them 'girls'.
And none of them have grown a beard;
We Dons, quite bluntly, think you're weird
And will not tolerate the view
That haute couture is good for you."
In short, de Hyde's defence had failed –
His days at Oxford were curtailed.
And that might well have been the end
Had Dominic not met a friend
Who offered him the perfect job
Where he could earn an honest bob.
For, through his chum, he gained admission
To the Equal Rights Commission –
A place where no one could care less
About the way employees dress.
Here, Dominic Formal de Hyde
Pronounces judgements that decide
When men and women are the same
(At least, I think that that's the aim).
So while he listens to the pleas
For equal opportunities
And equal pay and equal rights,
He wears his frock, his beard and tights.

QUENTIN COURTENAY CARADINE
Who was made an offer he couldn't refuse

A nauseating little swine
Was Quentin Courtenay-Caradine,
Who, as his name perhaps suggests,
Was one of Mother Nature's pests.
I met him first when I was small,
A meeting I can still recall,
For from the early age of three
The lad decided he would be
The sort of chap who makes life hell
And, goodness, he succeeded well.
A bully, sadist, snob and cad,
He was, to put it simply, BAD –
The sort of nasty thuggish brute
Whom secretly you'd like to shoot.
He ran our class with iron rule
And terrorised the Infant's School
(A leniently run Co-ed
With trendily progressive Head
Who 'spared the rod and spoiled the child'.
Result? Mixed Infants running wild).
The occupants of Class 5A
Were Cardine's especial prey –
He biffed us, bashed us, blacked our eyes,
(The lout was more than twice our size);
He stole our homework, tweaked our ears,
Reducing all of us to tears.
If anybody sneaked on him
He beat them up behind the gym;

And if this didn't get results,
He had twin-mounted catapults –
A weapon of his own design
That bought the rebels into line.
It was a simple step from here
To be a full-blown racketeer.
He ran a small gang of his own
Along the lines of Al Capone,
Extorting from us girls and boys
Our lunch allowance, Dinky Toys,
Pet spiders, marbles, model planes
And even Hornby Dublo trains.
He pinched our crayons, conkers and
A lot of other contraband
Like water pistols, bits of string,
Meccano sets – oh, anything
From rubber balls to sweets and nuts…
We absolutely loathed his guts.
We pandered to his every whim
For in return we got from him
The promise of protection from
A Courtenay-Caradine pogrom.
No teacher ever found him out.
Of this I've not the slightest doubt,
For written on his last report
Was "Good at lessons. Good at sport.
His grasp of everything is firm.
He's had a most successful term".

* * *

Now it was thirty years before
I came across the lad once more.
I saw a headline in *The Times*:
APPALLING CATALOGUE OF CRIMES
UNSCRUPULOUS AND VICIOUS LIES.
And there below, surprise, surprise,
The name of Courtenay-Caradine.
(It sent a shiver down my spine.)
But, oh, what bliss to see the wretch
Had earned himself a longish stretch
For burglaries and robbing banks
And other anti-social pranks.
The judge had told him that he should
Be locked up for the public good;
Which only goes to show us this:
Just how poetic justice is.

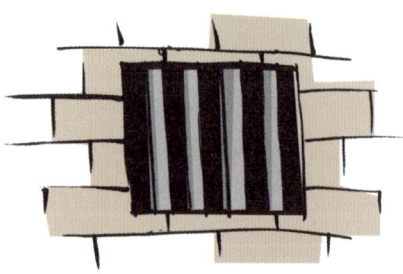

WILLIAM WINSTON EDWARD ROSE
Who did exactly that

William Winston Edward Rose
Is definitely one of those
Who by the happy chance of birth,
Are pre-ordained to rule the earth.
He knew this as a tiny boy.
His great-grandad (the Last Viceroy
Of some long-gone Protectorate)
Became a Minister of State
And then, amidst the National Cheers,
Ascended to the House of Peers –
Since when the Roses all have been
Advisors to the King or Queen.
So, William Rose (the youngest son
Of Geoffrey, Viscount Chippington)
Despite his lack of attributes,
Was sent to Eton, banked at Coutts,
And next was handed on a plate
A London house, a huge estate,
And, after scouring *Country Life*,
The dowry of his pretty wife
(A wealthy and attractive girl,
The daughter of an agèd earl).
A trust fund set up by his Pa
Was registered in Panama
Which hid his income from the view
Of HM Inland Revenue.

That's how he qualified to be
A good Conservative MP,
And now he's in the Cabinet
Demanding blood, toil, tears and sweat.
"Hard work," he says "is what we need
Before we're able to succeed.
Not one of us can live today
Unless we work to pay our way."

MUNROE McFITT

Who had lots of money but no fun

The miserly McFitts reside
Near Helensburgh on the Clyde.
'The Garth' is their detached abode,
In fact, it's some way from the road –
Forbidding, massive and austere,
The gates announce: GUARD DOGS LIVE HERE.
Surrounded by a twelve-foot fence
Electrified for self-defence,
'The Garth' was obviously designed
With frugal, feudal life in mind –
A cavernous and draughty pile
In pseudo-medieval style.
Ten bedrooms, all with bath en suite
Without the slightest bit of heat,
A dining hall, two kitchens and
Some furniture (all second-hand)

Combine successfully to give
A most unpleasant place to live.
An atmosphere of grim despair
Pervades the melancholy air
And every cold and draughty room
Is silent as a Pharaoh's tomb.
The postman treats it with respect
And few there are who would elect
To go within a mile of it,
For inside lives Munrow McFitt.
He made a fortune out of shipping,
Sacking men and asset-stripping.
He's got more money than Fort Knox
But wouldn't give you chicken-pox –
To get some money out of him
You'd have to tear him limb from limb.
He's stingy, niggardly and mean,
And so's his ghastly wife Eileen.
She also is immensely rich –
Descended from the Second Witch
Who met Macbeth in Shakespeare's play
(At least that's what the locals say).
They haven't got a lot of chums:
The Procurator Fiscal comes
To play the bagpipes once a year –
He used to be McFitt's cashier –
Strathspeys and reels, that sort of thing:
A somewhat gloomy highland fling.

This annual treat for the McFitts,
Thrills the pair of them to bits.
The pipes are all Munrow enjoys.
Apart from this distressing noise
He doesn't get much out of life
And certainly not from his wife.
He counts his money all alone –
No carpets, curtains, mobile phone,
Or ornaments and pictures which
Might indicate that he was rich.
A suit of armour, brown with rust,
A stuffed hyena, thick with dust,
Inherited from his Papa
Are all the *objets d'art* there are.
A misanthropic man is he –
A walking streak of misery.
There's one good thing that he achieves:
He lights a room up when he leaves.

PETER POPINJAY

Who pestered pets and prospered

To love our furred and feathered friends
Is something everyone commends.
However, Peter Popinjay
Is not disposed to feel this way.
To him, the only bird or beast
He likes is one that is deceased.

* * *

It started when the lad was two;
His Mummy took him to the zoo
To see the sea-lions for a treat –
She thought they would amuse young Pete.
Unfortunately for the pair,
A llama who was living there
Caught sight of Peter and his Mum
And, being somewhat troublesome,
He showed, by spitting llama phlegm,
Exactly what he thought of them.
The llama's unprovoked attack
Quite took the little lad aback
(And, frankly, one can sympathise –
It got him right between the eyes.)
From then on, every vertebrate
Became the object of his hate.

He started off with bugs and flies:
Oblivious to their insect cries
He pulled their legs off one by one
And found it was enormous fun.
Progressing rapidly to things
That flew with somewhat larger wings,
He shot down every passing sparrow
With his homemade bow-and-arrow.
His Dad exclaimed, "Cor, stone the crows!"
Said Pete, "That's just what I propose,"
And picking up a nearby brick
He muttered "This should do the trick."
Soon afterwards his parents saw
A sight that shook them to the core.
Their son had put inside a jar
The family's pet budgerigar.
He'd screwed the lid down tightly so
The budge couldn't say "Hello".
"You mustn't do that Pete," they said,
But by that time the bird was dead.
The next to suffer was the cat.
It made a useful cricket bat,
A handy ball, a pair of stumps…
It came up in all sorts of lumps.
Three overs later, it retired
And shortly after that expired.
His first report from school read: "He
Is brilliant at biology.

The boy is keen and quick to learn."
But soon this took a nasty turn –
A most unhealthy predilection
For the classes in dissection.
Cutting up dead frogs and cats,
Examining the spleens of bats
Is standard practice, it's the norm…
But not without some chloroform.
The teachers started taking bets
On why so many pupils' pets
Mysteriously went astray –
They smelt a rat, as one might say.
The odds on Popinjay were short;
Inevitably he was caught.
And what they found was quite grotesque,
For there, concealed inside his desk,
Were parts of the anatomy
Of several pets that used to be –
A skull, a scalpel and some fur…
They fetched the Head. "Excuse me, sir –
Alert the RSPCA!
We've found the culprit – Popinjay."
He was a murderous little bod,
A teeny-weeny Sweeney Todd.
Eventually he grew to be
A pillar of society –
A businessman of great renown
With interests in every town.

When next you pass a butcher's shop
And see some mincemeat or a chop
Remember Mr Popinjay
For he's provided the display.
His line of trade is wholesale meat
And every bit is killed by Pete:
He runs his abattoir with pride
And flogs the stuff off nationwide.
Yes, Peter Popinjay it is who
Caters for your joint or stew,
Your bacon, sausages and suet,
(Heavens! *Someone's* got to do it!)
He's tried to get permission to
Sell llama cutlets from the zoo
But no one there will let him harm a
Cuddly, lovely, little llama.
Still every week he goes to see
The llama in captivity;
Each week he brings a sharpened knife
And swears, "I'll have that llama's life."
And every week it is the same;
The llama treats it as a game:
It catches sight of him, then waits,
And, when in range, expectorates.

CYNTHIA SIMPSON

Who stuck it out to the bitter end

A habit that is commonplace is
Pulling lots of silly faces.
Cynthia Simpson found that she
Could do this most amusingly.
For once, when she was very young,
She found, by sticking out her tongue,
It did not only look quite rude, it
Was so long that it extruded
Right up to her nose's tip
(So handy, when it chanced to drip)
And down to just below her chin.
She hardly ever kept it in
But stuck it out at everyone –
Her school friends thought it heaps of fun.
She'd screw her face up, go cross-eyed
And wag her tongue from side to side,
Then hunch her back, and strike a pose,
Blow out her cheeks and lick her nose,
Or wave her hands and squint and leer
And make her eyeballs disappear –
A kind of facial acrobat.
Her Dad said, "It will stick like that.
You mark my words." "Oh phooey, Dad!"
Said Cynthia. But, next day, it had.

If only she had said "Okay"
She wouldn't have a lisp today.
She findth it hard to thay her name.
Her tongue thtickth out. Itth thuch a shame.
She altho hath to wear a bwathe
To keep pwotwuding teeth in plathe,
And whatth an even greater pity –
Thynthia thtarted out quite pretty.

ALEXANDER PHILLINOY

Who suffered a severe blow

A most revolting little boy
Was Alexander Phillinoy
Who, from his very early years,
(Without tuition it appears)
Developed with alarming zeal
A habit not at all genteel
Yet one which I must now disclose:
Young Alexander picked his nose.
The subject is distasteful, yes,
And Alex did it to excess.
At breakfast time, at lunch, at tea
Especially in company,
Whenever anybody looked
His thumb and finger would be hooked

Within the left- or right-hand hole;
And there he'd burrow like a mole.
He didn't care who saw him do it –
Picked it, scraped it, never blew it.
His parents did the best they could –
They smacked his hands; it did no good.
They told him it was not polite;
It was a truly awful sight.
They told him that a handkerchief
Was often used to bring relief
And that this small receptacle
Would help to hide the spectacle
(Which, quite apart from being rude,
Put both his parents off their food).
The more they pleaded and implored
The more young Alexander clawed
And scoured inside the dark abyss
That was his nasal orifice.
And what was more obscene and vile
Was watching Alexander while
He *looked* at what he'd excavated,
Licked it, liked it and then ATE it!
At length his father groaned, "Enough!
Here, Alexander, take some snuff!"
He begged his son on bended knees:
"Inhale it – it will make you sneeze.
And here's a handkerchief in case
You feel the need to wipe your face."

Young Phillinoy could not resist:
He scooped a pile up in his fist
And sniffed the snuff up in a trice
(A hundred grammes to be precise).
He stuffed the lot up all at once
Accompanied by snorts and grunts.
ATCHOO!! His father cried, "God bless!"
And then, "Oh dear, dear. What a mess."
ATCHOO!! A-A-T-CHOO!!! And then, "O Lor'!"
For red and shiny on the floor
They saw a sight at which they froze:
Alas! 'Twas Alexander's nose.
His Dad gasped, "Holy Moses, son!
You had two nostrils – now there's one!"
And sure enough, as black as coal,
There was, between his eyes, a hole.

* * *

His nose is now not on his face
But in a glass museum case.
It's mounted, with a silver plate
Inscribed:

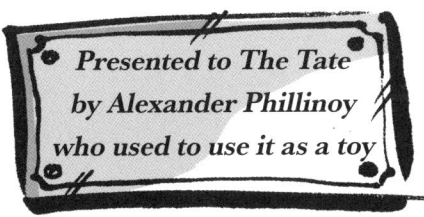

Presented to The Tate
by Alexander Phillinoy
who used to use it as a toy

A terrifying sight that's not
By any easily forgot.

Stop the Rot

Selected lyrics

'Stop the Rot' was what we affectionately called *Stop the Week*, the BBC Radio 4 programme hosted by Robert Robinson broadcast every Saturday evening from 1974 to 1992. For the 12 or so years I contributed to it, I wrote the lyrics and music of nearly 150 songs.

I landed the gig through the gifted singer and songwriter Peter Skellern who became not only a lifelong friend, but sang at our wedding and was godfather to our daughter. In 1972, he had had a big hit with *You're a Lady* – one of the truly great original pop songs – and in 1975 had co-written and performed in a mini-musical called *Loud Reports*. For the show's extended run, Skellern was unavailable. To replace him, they needed an actor who could play the piano.

Eventually, as our relationship developed and valuing his opinion, I plucked up the courage to sing some of my songs to him. He was not over-enthused by the serious stuff, but he seemed to like the others. At the time, he was writing two topical humorous numbers a week for *Stop the Week* (the two were soon reduced to one). With his pop career in the ascendancy, it became impossible for him to devote any time to the programme – which was when the producer, a suave Hungarian émigré named Michael Ember, decided to take a punt on Skellern's recommendation as his replacement: one month on, one month off, alternating with the likes of the groups Instant Sunshine and, latterly, Fascinating Aida.

The format of the programme was simple: each week a panel of four or five opinionated, witty, articulate speakers, drawn from a pool of regulars, would discuss a number of more or less frivolous topics. Subjects ranged from 'How to get rid of unwanted guests', 'Why are sandals wrong?' and 'The trouble with Volvo drivers' to 'Why are we so bad at the sports we invented?', 'Is it acceptable to floss in public?' and 'Buttons or zips?'

How it worked was like this: Ember would decide with Robinson on the topics to be discussed for the pre-recorded conversation (4.30pm, Friday, Broadcasting House). He would then ring me Thursday morning or afternoon to relay these topics around which the song might or might not be written – and to consider other subjects that I suggested. The lyrics would then be written during Thursday afternoon and evening, a short score of the music produced on Friday morning (piano, guitar, bass and drum kit) and then recorded at Broadcasting House after lunch, before Robinson and the regulars began filtering in from 4.00pm onwards. It's amazing what panic can inspire.

The tape of the new song would then be played in 'as live' half way through the chat to give everyone a breathing space. It was rare that Bob Robinson or any of the panel ever actually listened to the song – they still had the second half of the programme to fill with combative erudition, wit and wisdom. As Peter Skellern observed, one was merely the minstrel in the gallery. The selection of lyrics that follow had their origins in *Stop the Week* commissions but were often subsequently revised and polished.

NB: Song lyrics don't always read well on the printed page. Many of them benefit from being read aloud rather than in one's head. Others need the music to which they are eternally wedded for then to be fully appreciated. One thinks of the 'Hallelujah Chorus' from Handel's *Messiah*, or *All You Need Is Love* by The Beatles, neither of which look impressive on paper, but when sung… Just saying.

UNEXPECTED SHORTFALL

As the mortgage and the gas bills send me onward
To a kind of economic precipice,
I had a phone call from my banker.
Well, I couldn't have been franker
And the conversation went a bit like this…

I've got a cash flow problem at the moment,
My liquid assets seem to have run dry.
The position is one of monetary starvation
Which I shall do my level best to rectify.

It's an overdue non-payment situation
Which you've had the perspicacity to broach.
The overdraft and credit card repayments
Demand, I think, a flexible approach.

Your financial acumen is quite astounding.
I'm indebted for the interest you take.
The amount outstanding really has surprised me –
Are you sure you haven't made a slight mistake?

I hope that you won't mind me speaking bluntly.
It was awkward when my cheques began to bounce,
But, as you know, I feel that that speculative deal
Didn't really help to balance my accounts.

I anticipate an unexpected shortfall
Which will leave me slightly on the debit side.
There is a cheque due any day which will whittle it away
But until then I'm afraid my hands are tied.

No, it's not that I am unable or unwilling.
I would love to come and see you, were I free,
For your views on how I run my life in general
Have always deeply fascinated me.
The fact is, you and I are men of business
In a fluctuating, fickle marketplace,
So while I'm on the phone could you perhaps extend the loan
To afford me just a tiny breathing space?

I certainly don't want to sound ungrateful
But, although I owe the bank a tidy sum,
You'll have to damn well wait until I reaccumulate.
Till then you've got me by the short and curlies, chum.

TOKEN BOOKS

Since my schooldays I have struggled with the classics –
All those books that we were forced or told to read,
From the *Canterbury Tales* to *Prometheus Unbound*
From *De Bello Gallico* to *Adam Bede*.
Now I can do without T. E. and D. H. Lawrence
And you can stick Sir Walter Scott against a wall.
Away with Kafka, Baudelaire and burn James Joyce for all I care –

There are no pictures and the print is far too small.
Keep your Dumas and your Dantes,
All your Smolletts and Cervantes,
Stick your Plutarchs and your Pushkins in the bin.
I don't want to be depressed by
Mervyn Peake or Herman Hesse.
I don't want Schonberg! I want Gershwin and Berlin!

Give me some trash,
Give me a bash
At some total balderdash,
Give me a book that I can thoroughly enjoy.
It's getting tough
For I've had enough
Of all of that intellectual stuff
Where the subject matter soon begins to cloy.
Don't want problems!
All I want is fun,
Short chapters and the literary equivalent of the *Sun*.
Give me a paperback that's full of filth and hype,
Give me some lowest-common-denominator tripe.

When I unwind
I'm not inclined
To over-exercise my mind,
So I will read a book that I can finish soon.
Give me some grot!
Give me a plot
That's a load of tommy-rot!

Give me a library that's full of Mills and Boon!
Airport bookstalls
That's my kind of place.
Come out of the closet!
Pop a Cartland in your case!
Even a Jeffrey Archer, if you're in disguise –
Give me some thrills and spills and not the Booker Prize.

Give me some more
Of what I adore.
Dostoyevsky's such a bore
And George Eliot sends me rapidly to sleep.
Something that's strong –
You cannot go wrong
When most of the words are not too long
And there's nothing complicated or too deep.
A title such as *Lust* or *Grope* or *Greed*
Is all that's necessary for a novel to succeed.
A story with sex
And money reflects
The limit of what a reader expects,
So forget your Moby Dick and Westward Ho!
You can make quite a bit
If the author's a twit
And the book is a total load of shit.
I'm a publisher and I jolly well ought to know.

DOMESTIC DISPUTE

When I was a bachelor and lived alone
I didn't give a cuss.
I adamantly vowed that I'd
Remain polygamous.
I washed the dishes once a week
And lived the life of Riley
And looking back I cannot
Recommend that life too highly.
But other pleasures I have found
And my connubial bliss
Is only shattered when the
Conversation goes like this:

"Have you done the washing up?
For God's sake, wipe your feet!
Blow your nose! Don't pick it
While you're walking in the street!
Where's the money for the milkman?
God – I look a wreck!
I haven't any clothes to wear!
Please write me out a cheque.
Lay the table, clear the rubbish!
When you've finished that
Peel all those potatoes,
Walk the dog, then feed the cat!"

But I'm not nagged or hen-pecked –
No, I couldn't give a hoot,
For I clear the air by having a
Domestic dispute.

"Finish up your broccoli
And don't eat out of tins!
Clean the bathroom! Wipe your mouth!
And take your vitamins.
Turn the television down –
It's driving me insane!
For God's sake, do we have to have
Your parents here again?
Will you never volunteer to
Dust the kitchen shelf?
Am I to be expected to do
Everything myself?

Would you mind explaining, please,
The lipstick on your suit?"
It's then I know we're in for a
Domestic dispute.

"Tidy all those magazines!
My God, you drive me wild!
Clear up your Meccano and
Stop acting like a child.
Turn left! Turn left! I mean turn right!
Look out! The lights are red!
For God's sake, can't you think of
Anything but sex and bed?"
My wife's a perfect combination of a
Lover, friend and mother,

And what she says goes up one trouser
Leg and down the other.
In married life, I've found, there's one
Essential attribute:
Don't snigger when you're winning a
Domestic dispute.

TONGUE TWISTER

(sung to Rossini's La Danza*)*

If you've nothing to do for a minute or two
Then you might like to practice your speech.
Lots of people have tried it and many confided
Surprise at the standard they reach.
It's a wonderful thing to be able to sing
At the same time improving your diction.
Once your dentures are in, just relax and begin –
It will cure any vocal affliction.
Com-mun-i-cate!
Everyone knows what you're talking about.
Ar-tic-u-late!
Whether you whisper or stammer or shout.
Composers and writers have all tried to fright us
With patter songs, tongue twisters, poems and prose.
Your jaw becomes tense 'cos they never make sense,
But this is a hundred times better than those.

Especially good for impressing an audience –
Difficult passages sung without pause.
If you stop for a breath it'll just die a death
And prevent you from getting a round of applause.
"Sister Susie's sitting sewing shirts for sailors"
Is superficial
And a bit of a bore.
"Round the rugged rock the ragged rascal ran"
Is repetitious.
Need I say any more?
A glass of water can be quite an advantage.
Between the verses there is time for a sip.
So very soon now you can have a quick breather.
Whatever you do, though, you must not make a slip.

* * *

Intellectual smarties at dinners at parties
Will drive everybody insane.
Just by singing this ditty they'll say, "Oh, how witty –
You really must come round again!"
If you're making a speech or a lecture to teach
An ovation I'm sure you'll receive,
But forgetting a word needn't get you the bird –
Keep a copy of this up your sleeve.
You must not shun
(Please pay attention, I've not finished yet!)
El-o-cu-tion –

The more that you practice, the better you get.
The subject of money may strike you as funny
But writers must live, as I think you'll agree.
Before you perform, I'm afraid I must warn you to
Send me a cheque for a nominal fee.
I'm sure that Rossini would know what I mean as he
Made lots of money by writing this way.
He would knock off a tune before mid-afternoon
And then chat with his friends for the rest of the day.
"Betty bought a bit of butter but the butter
Betty bought was bitter"
Is a bit of a bore.
"Peter Piper picked a peck of pickled peppers"
Is pathetic.
Need I say any more?
And while you're singing you must never stop smiling
And give the impression you can do it with ease.
And when you're finished and completely exhausted,
Give a shrug of the shoulders, take a bow and say "Cheese!"

RHYMING CUTLETS

The animals went in two-by-two into Noah's Ark.
From then on, every animal has been left in the dark.
Do any of them find out what their farmyard lives are for?
Do you think that they discuss amongst themselves what lies in store?

Little sheep, little sheep,
After you have safely grazed,
Do you know that Bo-Peep
Will eat you roasted, grilled or braised?
I wonder what you're thinking
As your wool is shorn away?
Would you like to be a sweater
Or a frozen-food display?
Little hen, little hen,
I wonder how you're going to coop (sorry, cope)
Little ox, with your tail,
Soon you'll be a can of soup.
I wonder what you're thinking
When you see the auctioneer
With a metal earring up your nose
And a rosette in your ear.

Free range turkey, sheep or cows,
No matter where you roam
You're going to end up very close to
Bernard Matthews' home.
Little lamb, little lamb,

Soon you're going to be a chop.
Little pig – you'll be ham,
Reorganised in slices in a shop.
I wonder what you're thinking
Crowded in your cattle truck.
Your gambolling days are over now –
You'll have to take pot luck.

Little calf, little calf,
With your dark brown-eyed appeal –
You'll soon be wrapped in cellophane
In a package labelled 'veal'.
I wonder what you're thinking
As you chew the cud all day?
Would you be depressed to end as a
McDonald's take-away?

Sausage, cutlet, mincemeat, chop,
In the deep, deep-freeze,
Revenge is a dish that's best served cold:
It's called Mad Cow Disease.

FLIGHT OF FANCY

Check in nice and early, sir, departure is at one
So we'd like to have you standing by from eight.
We apologise to passengers – the flight will be delayed
And your baggage is ten kilos overweight.
Window seat or aisle, sir, or right above the wing
In a seat next to the fattest man in sight?
Let me search your luggage and your wallet and your crutch.
Hurry, or you're going to miss the flight!

Fasten your seat belts and turn off your mobile phones.
Don't even dream of lighting up a fag.
The oxygen mask is directly overhead.
If you're going to throw up, use this paper bag.
Leave all your belongings if the plane is forced to land
Mid-Atlantic or against a mountainside.
Exit doors are clearly marked and firmly locked, so please –
Relax, sit back, enjoy the ride.

Please ensure your seat is upright, briefcase on the floor,
Now wrap your arms and legs around your head.
Passengers in First Class will be served with pink champagne –
You can suck a boiled sweet instead.

That piece of yellow plasticine with cotton wool and paste
Is in fact the airline's complimentary meal.
Look down at the Pyrenees ten thousand feet below
While you're waiting for your coffee to congeal.

A small degree of turbulence is normal in this plane –
But the left-hand wing has worked a little loose.
You'll notice that the engine on the other side has stopped.
That's because we're running out of juice.
The flight has been diverted to Karachi. Never mind.
We'll play some soothing music which you'll like.
After we have landed, though, will passengers please note
That the baggage handlers here are all on strike.

The queue for checking passports is already round the block
And the temperature is 90 Fahrenheit.
Collecting your belongings from the baggage carousel
Will take about the same time as the flight.
Thank you all for flying with us, though we're quite amazed
That you put up with the service we provide.
In conclusion may I say how much our airline loves
Taking everybody for a ride.

GENERAL SYNOPSIS

The General Synopsis at 17:00
Was looking remarkably glum –
We'd been sailing round Britain for nearly a week
And we weren't sure which way we had come.
Then the Meteorological Office
Sent a map of the UK and France
Showing all the sea areas – terribly useful
To tell where you are at a glance.
So if you're adrift, feeling seasick,
Nail these words to the top of your mast
And decipher the General Synopsis
As you tune to the Shipping Forecast…

Off Norway, there's Viking and both the Utsires
Then Forties and Cromarty, Forth,
Down to Tyne, Dogger, Fisher and then German Bight –
Well, all those are roughly 'oop North'.
Coming south down the east coast are Humber and Thames,
And then for a while you're all right –
With the White Cliffs and tankers and cross-channel ferries
You pass on through Dover and Wight.
On to Portland and Plymouth, the Bay of Biscay

(Where it's choppy) just off the French coast.
If you shout "Ship ahoy!" then you'll be in Fitzroy
And at that point you'll be southernmost.

Turning north there is Sole to the south-west of Britain,
Then Lundy, Fastnet, Irish Sea.
On the west coast of Ireland there's Shannon and Rockall,
Then Malin – off Scotland ye'll be.
Up to Hebrides, Bailey, to Fair Isle and Faeroes,
(They're all pretty much the same thing).
When you reach South-East Iceland you'll take my advice and
Turn round, 'cos you've come a full swing.
Now we know where we're going, we'll just keep on rowing
Splice the mainbrace, my men! Homeward bound!
I think that I recognise where we are now.
Oh blast it! We've just run aground.

H²O

When you're hot and tired and dusty,
When your mouth is parched and dry,
When you're gasping for a drink of something wet,
When you're crossing the Sahara,
When you're miles from any Spa
A glass of H²O has not been bettered yet.

Give me some water, water, water!
Give me a drink!
Show me a hose-pipe, fountain, trough,
A bottle or sink!
Yes, give me a tap-full of the stuff
'Cos I can never get enough
Of that A-B-C-D-E-F-G- H²O.

I've got water on the brain –
Pass it, flush it, pull the chain!
There's such a lot of things that it can do.
I'll guarantee you'll love it –
Just keep your head above it,
Water-pistol, water-closet, Waterloo.

Give me a glass of H²O
As clear as a bell.
Show me a spring, a river
Or artesian well.
H²O makes my mouth water –
Oh how I wish that I had brought a
Tank of A-B-C-D-E-F-G- H²O.

* * *

When you've opened your umbrella,
When it's time to take a bath,
When you're trying to be a flower or a tree,
When a silver cloud is whining
'Cos it hasn't got it's lining,
Without water...well, you couldn't even pee.

You need water, water, water,
A puddle or lake.
Show me a tea-bag, kettle
Or a duck without a drake!
Show me a hippo and a drought
And without the slightest doubt
They'll want A-B-C-D-E-F-G- H_2O.

Put me on the wagon
With some Vichy in my flagon!
I'm off to Carlsbad for my holiday.
No, it don't mean a thing
If it ain't got that spring –
Baden-Baden, Buxton, Perrier...

You gotta have water, water, water,
A drop or a drip.
Give me something with splash and splosh
I can swill or swig or sip!
There's only one thing doesn't suit it –
That's when you try to dilute it.
Give me A-B-C-D-E-F-G- H_2O,
I want A-B-C-D-E-F-G- H_2O,
I love A-B-C-D-E-F-G- H_2O.

PRESIDENTIAL PRECEDENTS

(The introduction is sung to The Battle Hymn of the Republic*;
the verses are set to* Marching Through Georgia *and* Dixie*)*

The Presidents of the United States democracy enshrine,
But there's now been more than forty of them since 1789.
In fact, so many that no-one can remember who they were –
So here's a chronological list to which you can refer.

First was old George Washington, the man who never lied,
John Adams, Thomas Jefferson, then Maddison (who died).
Munroe and Quincy Adams, Andrew Jackson, Van Buren,
William H. Harrison and Tyler make it ten.
In 1845 came Polk (whose middle name was Knox)
And four years later Zachary Taylor won the ballot box.
Americans love Presidents with silly-sounding names,
So next were Millard Fillmore, Franklin Pierce, Buchanan (James).
Then Lincoln came in '61 – a great man, I confess –
(I wonder, should I send this to his Gettysburg address?).
Andrew Johnson, Grant and Hayes with Garfield make a score,
We've also reached the half-way point. Let's stop then have some more!

The President in '81 was Chester Arthur, then
Came Grover Cleveland, Harrison and Cleveland once again.
McKinley, Teddy Roosevelt and Taft in nineteen-nine,
Woodrow Wilson was for years the nation's valentine.
Coolidge followed Harding and then Hoover swept to power,
Next Franklin Roosevelt, Truman and then Dwight D. Eisenhower.
With Kennedy and Lyndon Johnson, Nixon, Gerald Ford,
Then Carter, Regan, Bush (the father) on the honours board
Succeeded by Bill Clinton and George Dubya Bush (the son),
Obama, Trump and now Jo Biden. That's the lot! We're done!

PUB CRAWL

I popped out for a drink last night down at the Barley Mow,
A public house with old-world atmosphere.
I played a game of skittles there then, by the open fire,
I sat and drank a nice cool pint of beer.

It wasn't long before I went up for another pint
And after that I think I had one more.
A fella bought me one or two and then I bought him one
And then we had another three or four.

CHORUS (straight)
Raise your glasses, drink a toast,
God Save the Queen and Cheers,
Here's looking at you, all the best old son!
Well, bottoms up, good health, chin-chin,
God bless and down the hatch!
No please, it's my turn. Let me get this one.

* * *

Next I called in for a minute at the Rising Sun.
I had a pint but didn't like it there.
So I moved on to the White Horse Inn and then the Bull and Bush
And ended up inside the Fox and Hare.

I bumped into a friend of mine – we had a pint or two –
But the piano in the bar was out of tune.
So we settled in the Anchor, had some lager for a change
And played a game of darts in the saloon.

CHORUS (slightly slurred and staccato)

* * *

We called in at the Lamb and Flag and then the Plough and Stars
And had a pint of Guinness at The Bell.
We had a gin and tonic with the barmaid at The Cock
Where she serves hand-pumped and home-brewed beer as well.

We listened to the jukebox while we sipped another pint
Before we thought we'd try the Prince of Wales.
We went into the snuggery and half an hour later
We had sampled half a dozen of their ales.

CHORUS (dishevelled, noisy, amiable)

* * *

My friend said we should pay a visit to the Cat and Fiddle
Where they kept a glass of cider in its prime.
So after three or four of those I said we'd better hurry –
It was getting rather near to closing time.

We swiftly downed another pint, arriving just in time
To get last orders at the Spotted Dick,
But we didn't like the fruit machine, the landlord or the beer,
So it was there that we decided to be sick.

CHORUS (incomprehensible)
(Spoken: "Time gentlemen, please!")

UNDERGROUND HYMN

(to be sung to the hymn tune 'Austria' by Haydn)

Journey on the Metropolitan
Piccadilly, Jubilee
District, Central and Victoria,
Bags of fun and all for free:
Vault the automatic barriers
(It's a cinch at Kentish Town)
Then run up the escalators
While the stairs are going down.

Spend a day with London Transport
Underneath this town of ours.
Catch a Circle Line to anywhere –
Then go round and round for hours.
Stand well clear of platform edges!
Doors are closing! Mind the gap!
Talk to strangers, sing and whistle,
Then go and sit on someone's lap.

On the Bakerloo and Northern
Certain special rules apply.
Standing on the left's obligatory –
Make sure no one can get by.
If you are a foreign student
With a back-pack and a case,
You must travel in the rush hour
When there isn't any space.

Tooting Broadway, Chalfont Latimer,
Headstone Lane and Northwood Hills –
Distant outposts of the Underground
Guaranteed for cheap day thrills.
Note the very fine graffiti at
Gospel Oak, which must be seen,
And the pungent smell of lavatories
As you enter Parsons Green.

If you think you know your Underground
Here's a quiz to test your skill :
Where are Fairlop, Debden, Alperton,
Boston Manor, Buckhurst Hill?
Did you know that Greenford, Moor Park,
Barking, Balham, Tottenham Hale,
Seven Sisters and South Ruislip
Interchange with British Rail?

If you think that pigs and cattle are
Treated different from the rest,
Half-past-five from Oxford Circus will
Put your theory to the test.
Yet despite its imperfections
No alternative has been found
Should you wish to traverse London
In a tunnel underground.

VALENTINE CARD

Why do I love me?
Hook, line and sinker it just had to be,
For can't you see?
How could I decline
When I asked me to become my Valentine?
I send a shiver up and down my spine,
Can't take my eyes off me.

Demurely I avert
My loving gaze from me – it's cruel to flirt...
I might get hurt.
So simply, entre nous,
From now on I promise me that I'll be true,
But that's not hard to do –
No longer slighted
Or unrequited
Who says that Love is blind?
I know my ego
Is my amigo –
Oh what a lucky find!

Who is this I see
Peeping round the bathroom door alluringly?
Oh gosh! It's me!
Frankly, I am blessed –
I take a selfie when I get undressed
And, boy, am I impressed.
Can't take my eyes off me.

Several in the past
Thought they'd stay the distance but were all outclassed
This time it's going to last.
I'm the groom and bride...
Only took a moment for me to decide
And when I did – I cried.
No more temptation,
Just pure elation
Each time I catch my eye.
My troth's been plighted.
I'm so excited
Now I'm a one guy guy.

BRIEF ENCOUNTERS

I'll tell the story of a boy called Ted born in 1943.

His middle names were Bob and Dick. He was baptised C of E.

He never met his father in the BEF abroad,

Fighting off the SS and the German Nazi horde.

So his mother took in PGs just to help her through the War.

They were GIs from the USA – I hardly need say more.

With her hubby out at HQ, well it caused her some distress

That she got herself in trouble years before the NHS.

So the GP came when Ted was born but, lacking LSD,

His mum sold Ted for fifty bob and on the strict QT.

His new dad was a VIP – Sir Francis Thurley, Bart.,

A JP and a millionaire. He gave Ted quite a start,

For Frank became a KCB and friends with the PM.

His greatest chum was HRH – the top crème de la crème.

Ted didn't want for anything and went to public school.

He got nine Os and then three As – so not a bloody f… (sorry! BF).

He went to university and got a Ph.D,

Then married fellow-student Liz, a first class B.Sc..

They had three bonny little lads called Tel and Al and Pete

And though they're rather non-U names, they're really awfully sweet.

Liz has got a high IQ and is very OSP.

She joined the local WI and did the VAT.

And as for Ted, he ended up no less the man i/c

Of editing abbreviations for the OED.

Just to make it clear – 'Os' refer to 'O-Levels;' the precursors of GCEs

and 'As' refer to 'A-Levels' (Ed)

CAMPING OUT

Once I was a Boy Scout
And I knew lots and lots –
I could put a broken leg in splints
And tie all sorts of knots.
I smiled and whistled all the time
And got my Bushman's Thong,
So when I became a Queen's Scout
I sang this camping song. . .

CHORUS Can you get your tent pole up in the dark?
When you rub two sticks together make them spark?
Shalla-wally-shalla-wally-oompah
Keep your woggle in your hand,
Shalla-wally-shalla-wally, Be Prepared,
The camping life is grand.
Have you ever managed putting up a tent
In a howling gale when all the guys are bent?
Snuggled in our sleeping bags by the fireside,
I will do the scouting, if you will be the guide.

The outdoor life's a challenge
To Boy Scouts or Marines –
Climbing up a mountainside
Or digging the latrines.
When your feet are tired and aching
After walking forty miles,
All you ask for is a groundsheet
To stop you getting pi. . . damp.

CHORUS (as above)

Camping is a man's life
And camping out is tough –
Baden-Powell, the Wolf Cub Howl
And all that Gang Show stuff.
Sleeping under canvas
In the snow and wind and rain,
How it warms a fellow's cockles
To sing the old refrain.

CHORUS (as above)

And now I'm not a Boy Scout –
I haven't camped for years.
Instead I go on package tours
To Bangkok or Tangiers.
No longer do I camp about
Inside a bivouac
And the words of our old camping song
Don't easily come back.

CHORUS I can't get my tent pole up in the dark.
When I rub two sticks I cannot make them spark.
Shall-wally-shalla-wally-oompah
Now it's hard to understand
Shalla-wally how I ever kept my woggle in my hand,
How I ever managed putting up a tent
In a howling gale when all the guys were bent.
The only sleeping bag I've got is by the fireside –
Now she doesn't like me scouting
And she doesn't want to guide.

GOSH, IT WAS FUN

We've just returned from a fabulous spot –
Over the seas we fly –
All things considered, it cost quite a lot –
Sun, sand and clear blue sky.
I took a T-shirt and one pair of shorts
(Enough for a fortnight's stay).
She took a dozen bikinis and two different
Dresses for every day.
Got to the airport at just before dawn
And took off at quarter-past-two.
She was on Valium, I was gin
And so were the pilot and crew.

Gosh, it was hot! Gosh, it was fun!
What a wonderful time we had there.
I must say the earthquake was quite an event –
And so was the cholera scare.

At the Hotel Paradiso, we found –
Over the seas we fly –
None of the toilet facilities worked –
They'd cut off the water supply.
'Night Life' they promised us in the brochure
And 'a room with a beautiful sight'.
Builders worked on the site most of the day
And the disco beneath us all night.

Nobody seemed to speak English at all,
The waiters were robbing us blind,
Our travellers' cheques disappeared by the pool
But, honestly, we didn't mind, 'cos...

Gosh, it was hot and gosh, it was fun!
We've booked up again for next year
In spite of the fact we spent most of the time
With unusually bad diarrhoea.

First I went pinkish, then I went red –
Over the seas we fry –
Then I got sunstroke and then my skin peeled
With blisters and bites on my thigh.
Took us an hour to walk to the beach,
Which became just a bit of a drag.
Wrote you a card saying 'Wish you were here' –
And the postcard is still in my bag.
When we got back, it was raining and cold
(At least we weren't hi-jacked mid-air!).
Then we got home and we found that the house
Had been burgled, but we didn't care, 'cos...

Gosh, it was hot! Gosh, it was fun!
Though I've still got a bad stomach ache,
Once I've caught up with some sleep I can say
"It was worth it, I needed the break."

I CAN'T QUITE REMEMBER YOUR NAME

Oh, I say! There's that girl with Vanessa –
I don't think she's spotted me yet.
She's a girl I adore – yes, I've met her before –
But there's one tiny problem I cannot ignore
And it brings me out into a sweat...

I know that we met at a party last year
But I can't quite remember your name.
You like listening to Poulenc and Satie – it's queer
But I just can't remember your name.
I remember your scent and the touch of your lips,
And the way you liked eating asparagus tips.
I'm afraid that my memory's to blame
But I can't quite remember your name.

Was it Cleo or Clara or Chloe?
Was it Cathy or Carrie I kissed?
Perhaps it was Fanny...or maybe Fiona,
I wish that I'd made out a list.

A friend said your father was wealthy as Croesus.
Why can't I think of your name?
You went to Girton and I went to... *Jesus*!
Why can't I think of your name?
I remember your birthday, your Zodiac sign,
Your telephone number – six-eight-double-nine.
But my memory has put me to shame,
'Cos I can't quite remember your name.

Is it Beatrix, Brenda or Bridget?
My address book I really should bring.
Oh, I know! She's the daughter of... what is he called?
If I ask her, I'll blow the whole thing.

I know that you came back to my place that night
But I can't quite remember your name.
You asked me to get out and turn off the light.
I still can't remember your name.
We woke up next morning and drank some champagne
And though it is lovely to see you again
I suspect that you're thinking the same –
'Cos you can't quite remember my name...
I know where I met her, I'd never forget her,
Now all I can do is exclaim:
(SPOKEN) "Hallo, darling! How are you?"
Gosh, I hope I remember her name.

THE NIGHT THAT WE DINED
AT THE BEETONS'

Nigella Lawson and Delia Smith,
Gordon Ramsay – you cannot deny
Are all quite at home on the range, they say,
And can bake, boil, simmer and fry.
But we had a meal a few weeks ago
That left all these cooks quite out-chef'd.
We sat down to eat at a quarter-to-eight;
It was just after two when we left.

Oh, the night that we dined at the Beetons'
We had such a jolly good nosh.
We started with *Consommé à la Brunoise*
And ended with *Chocolate brioches.*
We had *Poulet en casserole, Crème de volaille*
And *Concombre à la poulette.*
There was *Choufleur au gratin* and *haricots verts*
With *Turbot bouillisce aux crevettes.*
We had *Pigeons en compote* and *Mignons de veau*
With *Cardon au jus* and *croquettes,*
Plus the *Choux de Bruxelles à la maître d'hotel*
And some *Pommes frites* and *Sauce vinaigrette.*
After that we had *Boeuf braisé à la bourgeoise*
And then I was ready for pud.
I didn't know what I was eating at all,
But, by golly, it wasn't half good.

After all that, I was full of regard
For our hostess's tour de force.
I had folded my napkin, when more food arrived
And I doubted if I'd stay the course.
"Oh, there's plenty more yet," Mrs. Beeton announced,
As she served me a lemon sorbet.
"I hope you'll allow that you can't give up now
When I've slaved in the kitchen all day."

Oh, the night that we dined at the Beetons'
The food was a bit of all right.
For dessert we had *Tartelettes d'épines-vinettes*
With a topping of *Angel Delight*,
Meringues à la crème and *Champignons farçis*,
Then *Macedoine de fruits en gelée*,
Accompanied by a *Soufflé de semoule*
And a *Glacé aux amandes brûlés*.
Croustades de Parmesan, Crème au fromage,
Bouchées de caviar too,
But after the *Canapés à la Française*
I had to admit I was through.
"Mr. Beeton," I said, over port and cigars,
"Your wife, sir, can certainly cook."
"That's all very well," he replied, "but, oh hell,
Now she's thinking of writing a book."

OPEN WIDE

I love to feast on caramel,
Fudge, marzipan and cake.
Last week, while eating walnut whirls,
A tooth began to ache.
It started getting painful
When I ate some chocolate spread,
So I went to see a dentist chap
And this is what he said:

Open wide! Open wide!
And let's see what you've got there inside.
My goodness me, it's not a pretty sight
Which isn't helped by what you dined on last night –
Garlic bread, I should guess,
Rack of lamb with some mustard and cress.
The fillings in your upper mouth are fairly antique –
An area that's clearly not been brushed for a week.
That and cigarettes incline to make your breath reek.
Open wide, open wide, open wide!

Open wide! Open wide!
Oh hello, what is this that I've spied?
Three hearty cheers! Hip, hip, hooray!
I've found a largish tract of tooth decay.
Oh what fun! What a thrill!
Now at last I can get out my drill.
A local anaesthetic would be nice, I admit,
But without one (though it might hurt just a wee tiny bit)
It's easier to find out what the hell I have hit.

Open wide, open wide, open wide!
I lay back horizontally,
He sat down by my side.
He asked me if I felt alright
And I of course replied,
"I'll give up eating nougat, toffee, *
Chocs and coffee cream." *
But he didn't seem to hear me
And continued with his theme...

Open wide! Open wide!
Oh, I hope that my hand doesn't slide.
If it's uncomfortable, please let me know
Because the drill I use is rather slow.
Hold this tube. It will suck
The saliva, the blood and the muck.
My guide dog's in the next room! That's an old dentists' joke.
But do try not to swallow, will you? There's a good bloke.
Just signal with your hand when you're beginning to choke.
Open wide, open wide, open wide!

Open wide! Open wide
As the drill and the nerve-end collide.
I beg you, don't attempt to scream or speak
Or I might slip and go right through your cheek.
Read *The Times* and relax
As I bung up the holes and the cracks.
I'll just extract that molar 'cos it is a bit loose
And your wisdom teeth as well, which frankly aren't any use.
Now sit upright, rinse your mouth and spit them out in the sluice.
Open wide, open wide, open wide!

(*spoken as with mouth full of drill and cotton wool)

PLACE SETTINGS

Sheila's next to Andrew and Andrew's opposite Marge,
Sarah can have the window seat because she's rather large.
Clive can flirt with Kay, so put Sally on the right.
Kath must be with Ian 'cos he's bound to end up tight.
Edward can go in the corner – I'm sure he wouldn't mind.
Bill can talk the pants off Jim, let Joy be unconfined.
Dorothy's a problem because she's such a bitch.
On the other hand, she's very old and very rich.

Susan has decided she's going to come with Kim
And Bertram is insisting that we put him next to Tim.
Philip and his girl-friend won't come with any luck –
They've got so much in common. Yes, they're both as common as muck!
Simon can cope with Nicky as long as she's not near Ted,
So we'd better put Ken with Antonia after what Elspeth said.
But Dorothy's a problem – she's such a frightful bore.
Her cystitis is still playing up so put her near the door.

Jill has rung to tell me that she fancies Dick,
But he's a friend of Dorothy's – I don't think they would click.
Shall we ask the Wilsons? Would it be all right
If we took them into the garden and kept them out of sight?
Chelsea, Wayne and Kayleigh *** will have to sit next to their Mum.
As long as I'm nowhere near them, we'd better let them come.
But Dorothy's a problem – she's got a frightful thirst,
She eats us out of house and home and always gets here first.

Martin's next to Tina and Tina's such a tease.
Keep her away from Elizabeth or it's bound to upset Louise.
Cyril and Natasha have said they'll try and show,
But they don't get on with David, Richard, Angela or Joe.
Jean-Pierre and Martina are flying in from France.
Shall we keep a place for them or shall we take a chance?
But Dorothy's a problem – she's coming on her own.
Reg put up with her last time – let's give her Aunty Joan.

I think that's everybody – there's you and me, my dear.
Oh wait! We've left out * * * *. They'll have to come next year.

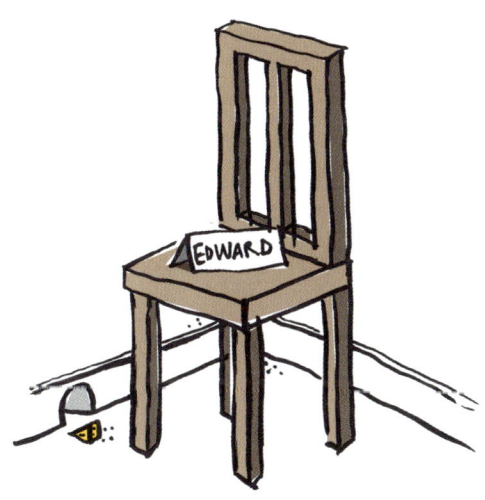

***Or: Hamlet and Ophelia

**** insert anybody who you want to embarrass

PRETTY PLAIN

Beauty's in the eye of the beholder –
As we grow older
It's pretty plain.
Every mirror now reflects
So much less than one expects –
It's pretty plain.
La Gioconda has lost her charm
(It's no use moaning, Lisa),
Venus de Milo has lost an arm
And no one wants to squeeze her.
And yet . . .
And yet . . .
In my best bib and tucker
I'm not finished yet . . .

My God, I look lovely tonight!
What a sight!
What a dazzling, resplendent delight!
It's exquisite!
My word!
It's absurd
That this beautiful creature is me!
I look lovely tonight.

Some say that my bald patch is sexy –
To cover it up is an art –
Yellowing teeth can be polished, they say,
And they tell me gold fillings look smart.

My figure of breath-taking slimness
Is no longer so lissom or svelte.
My umbilical knot is disguised by a pot
And it hangs out the side of my belt.

But my God I look lovely tonight!
Dynamite!
And I think that I very well might
Give a cheer.
For despite
All my faults
I'm as suave as a Viennese waltz –
I look lovely tonight.

* * *

I don't think I really need glasses,
But I bought a pair just for a lark.
My darling complains that my varicose veins
Are like roadmaps to read in the dark.

My ingrowing toenail's a nuisance,
So's the wart that's come up on my chin.
There's not much I can risk since I had my slipped disc
But I struggle on through thick and thin.

My God, I look lovely tonight!
Well, quite.
I admit that my shirt collar's tight.
Never mind,
I look chic
And so sleek
With my tongue firmly tucked in my cheek
I look lovely tonight.
I think Aphrodite
And Helen of Troy might be
Smitten and fairly impressed.
But please,
On my knees,
Don't let them see me undressed!

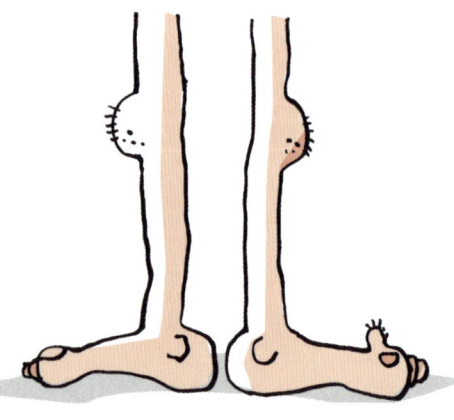

SNOW FEVER

(with apologies to John Masefield)

I must go out to the shed again for another bucket of coal.
For some fur-lined boots and an anorak I would sell my soul.
And all I ask is the plumber will come round this afternoon
And the burst pipe in the bathroom will be mended soon.

I must go up to the loft again, to make it waterproof,
For I have to replace the tiles where the snow's come through the roof
And all I ask is a telephone man will turn up here,
Then I can ring for the central-heating engineer.

I must go out to the car again, though it's twenty degrees below.
I don't know where I should start to dig for it's buried under the snow.
And all I ask when the battery's flat in a howling Arctic breeze,
Are some jump leads and the A.A. and some antifreeze.

I must go down to the station now – I'll have to try, at least –
But the trains haven't run for a fortnight now and it's difficult on the piste.
And all I know is that nothing will change, so have no fear –
We'll all be totally unprepared when it snows next year.

USHERETTE'S BLUES

I work at the Palace Cinema
As an usherette, you know,
And I've been tearing tickets there
For fifty years or so.
Showing people to their seats
And selling the ice-creams –
The Palace is a wonderland
Of fantasy and dreams.
I get to see the films for free
But it drives me round the bend –
Because I am an usherette
I never see the end…

Did Gary Cooper get the girl, or what?
Did Judy Garland find her dog?
Were Robert Redford and Paul Newman shot?
Did Snow White turn into a frog?

I don't know if the Phantom showed his face
Or if they captured Orson Welles.
Did Charlton Heston win the chariot race?
Did they let Charles Laughton keep his bells?

I'd love to know what happened to King Kong
And whether Bonny married Clyde.
Did Julie Andrews sing another song?
And was Kirk Douglas crucified?

Did Indiana ever find The Ark? –
Oh, how I love the silver screen! –
In Jaws, did anybody catch that shark?
I've missed the end of every film I've seen.

How *Star Wars* ends I haven't got a clue,
I sat through most of *Spinal Tap*,
I saw two-thirds of *Terminator Two*
And lots of other total junk.
Don't spoil the ending, but I kinda feel
That Kate and Leonardo drown.
Now just today I've watched my final reel –
Next week they're going to pull the Palace down.

THE LOST CHORD FOUND
(with absolutely no apology to Adelaide Proctor)

Seated one day at the Steinway
I began to compose a piece –
Would it be an Intermezzo,
Prelude or Valse-Caprice?
I improvised first in E flat
And changed key into A,
Then I struck one chord of music
And it would not go away,
No, it would not go away.

I hated the sound that chord made
And yet it stuck in my brain.
I tried playing something in waltz time
But back it came again.
I stopped extemporising
And played some Bach instead,
But whatever I seemed to turn
That chord ran through my head.

I tossed off the Liszt Sonata,
Played a Chopin waltz or two,
Then sight-read *Gaspard de la Nuit*
And *Rhapsody in Blue*.
With some strange premonition
I turned to another score
And started to play a selection
From *H.M.S.Pinafore…*

I went through the opening number
And reached the first refrain.
My concentration wandered
And I struck that (!) chord again.
I rose with a shriek of anguish
At the sound the piano made,
For I realised that the chord was the one
That Sullivan mislaid.

WE'RE HAVING A SOIRÉE THIS EVENING

We're having a soirée this evening.
I'll tell you who is going to be there:
Diana and Gerald, the Featherstonehaughs, the Mackies
And Bunty and Betty Adair.
It's not very often we do this
But this one's a really big 'do'.
We've hoovered and dusted and polished all over
And put some new soap in the loo.
We've been slaving all day in the kitchen.
We'll be just about ready on time.
I daren't even think what it's cost us –
The price of champagne is a crime.
We've got out the cut glass and silver,
There's plenty of ice in the fridge,
We've got out the cards and the pencils
In case some of them want to play bridge.
They're going to arrive any minute.

I wonder who is going to be first?
The Featherstonehaughs are quite heavy going.
Once they're here, we'll be over the worst.
I admit I'm a little bit nervous –
I do hope it goes well tonight.
I've had a few sherries to steady myself
And I think I'm a little bit tight.

* * *

My God, what a dreadful disaster!
My God, what a terrible night!
No one turned up! They all cancelled!
How *could* they be so impolite?
Not one of them actually made it.
Not one of them actually came.
They all phoned to say they weren't coming
And the reasons were terribly lame.
Diana said Gerald had measles,
The Adairs (from what I could deduce)
Had been struck with some form of amnesia
Or some such unlikely excuse.
The Featherstonehaughs say I didn't ask them,
Which I know is an out-and-out lie
And the Mackies phoned up from a call box
To pretend they were still up in Skye.

They stood us up at the last minute.
I'm fed up and nearly distraught.
How frightfully thoughtless and rude of our friends
After all of the food that we've bought.
It's no use denying I'm sulking.
I'll sit down and watch the TV.
I wonder why everyone cancelled?
But wait! What is this that I see?
Oh, thank goodness – it's only just started.
Thank God that they didn't turn up.
I'd have missed all of *Strictly Come Dancing*.
Now that really would make me fed up!

ODE TO BE IN ENGLAND

In England's pleasant pastures green
Where the Yorkshire pudding grows
And the Betjeman blossoms wherever you look
And the bowler hats peacefully doze,
Where the sun shines forth on clouded hills
At least three days of the year
And the Armstrong Siddeley Sapphire snoozes
After a pint of beer,
From down in the Vale of Evesham,
To the Pennines, the Mendips and Lakes,

The natives go gathering bunches of Elgar
And bouquets of Churchills and Drakes.

CHORUS So O to be in England,
For Englishmen live there –
Eccentric, bloody-minded, yes,
But scrupulously fair.
They clean the bath out after use,
They're loyal, bold and straight,
But, most important, always let
Their elbows take the weight.

This precious stone set in the silver sea
Where the kedgeree gambols and skips
And the marmalade blooms with the bacon and eggs
And the rivers have fishes and chips.
By the side of a stream or a babbling brook
In some corner of any old field,
It is fairly well-known that umbrellas are grown
And rice pudding is often congealed.
From down by the White Cliffs of Dover,
By the Severn, the Mersey and Trent,
Picking the Fortnum and Masons will be
That broad-shouldered, genial gent. [9]

CHORUS (as before, but with even more patriotic pride)

There'll always be an England
Where the Noël Cowards sing
In the forests of Brylcreem and ketchup
Where the Corbyn reigns as king.

[9] Isn't that a line from Tennyson? (Ed.) Yes. (JN)

Where Ascot means horses and heating
And the wind in the Boris field blows
In the land full of 2 point 4 children
And the pubs are too early to close.
From Margate and Malvern to Marlow
And from Stafford to Stow-on-the-Wold
There are Englishmen breeding their Kipling and Wrens,
Self-effacing, self-made, self-controlled.

CHORUS (*con nobilmente* and extra passion and fervour)

SNIP SNIP

Every month I pay a visit to the barber's shop.
A shampoo from a nice young girl, then a little off the top.
The shampoo girl is lovely – I like her gentle touch.
I'm sure I'd like the barber too, if he didn't talk so much.

Snip!
Nice to see you, sir. Please take a seat.
Snip snip!
Ain't it awful for the time of year?
Snip snip!
Would you like a trim or shall I take it
Snip!
Half an inch or so above the ear?

Snip!
We haven't seen you for a time.
Snip snip!

Month or two? I can't remember when.
Snip snip!
Did you want to have your sideboards off, sir?
Snip!
Never mind. I'm sure they'll grow again.

Snip!
Have you heard the one about the nun?
Snip snip!
Hold it steady, sir, and face the front.
Snip snip!
Who the devil cut your hair last time, sir?
Snip!
'Cos his scissors were a trifle blunt.

I listen to his idle chatter, though he doesn't concentrate.
My hairstyle would have been in vogue in 1958.
He always cuts it much too short in spite of what I say.
The bits get in my collar and there's quite a lot to pay...[10]

Snip!
What about that match last night!
Snip snip!
And the referee they had – oh dear!
Snip snip!
Tell me if I'm taking too much off, sir.
Snip!
Whoops! Sorry, did I clip your ear?

Snip!
Have you ever thought about a wig?

[10] Is this a deliberate pun? (Ed.) Yes (JN)

Snip snip!
Getting just about as thin as mine.
Snip snip!
Got a customer as bald as Kojak
Snip!
In every Monday for a buff and shine.

Snip!
Did you see that on the box last night?
Snip snip!
Did you really? Well, I never did.
Snip snip!
All done, sir! Looking very smart again!
Snip!
Special price to you – just fifty quid.
Anything for the weekend, sir?

HIT LIST

(Parody of 'As someday it may happen' from The Mikado, *with apologies to G&S)*

If anybody asks me what annoys me nowadays,
I've made little list, I've made a little list
In the form of an affectionately-written paraphrase
Of a certain lyricist. I'm sure you've got the gist!
There's the teenage motorcyclist who will never pass his test
On a bike that rattles party walls and thinks that we're impressed.
Those people on their mobile phones who chatter on the train
And who'd smash your face in if you have the courage to complain.
The platitudes of politician and trade unionist.
They'd none of them be missed. They'd none of them be missed.

CHORUS I've got 'em on the list, I've got 'em on the list
And they'll none of them be missed. They'll none of them be missed.

There's the pseudo-intellectual who shows off with quotes and facts.
He simply can't resist – I've got him on the list –
And the man to whom twice yearly I am forced to pay my tax.
I know that I'd be missed if I wasn't on his list.
There's the chap who never listens who's the dinner-party bore
And the feminist who doesn't thank you when you hold the door,
The idiots on motorways who drive ten feet behind
And are either suicidal, drunk or absolutely blind
With silly stickers on the rear: the manic motorist.
I don't think he'd be missed. I know he'd not be missed.

CHORUS Yes I've got him on the list, I've got him on the list
And don't think he'd be missed. I'm sure he'd not be missed.

Those people who to concerts go to cough and clear the throat.
Though I'm a pacifist, I'd like to use my fist.
And experimental music that requires a programme note –
There's another on my list: the modern symphonist.
All discotheques, computer games and people who jump queues,
And the chap who does *The Times* crossword and answers all the clues.
All those who moan about a programme but don't switch it off,
And the paparazzi – bottom of the journalistic trough –
And, finally, the writer who's a downright plagiarist!
They'd none of 'em be missed. They'd none of 'em be missed.

CHORUS There are two names on the list
that you might think I have missed,
But without them I am certain that this song would not exist.

HUGGER MUGGER

I've got a little something here
You might quite like to see,
Top secret, off the record
And confidentially.
It's not for publication,
So just keep it up your sleeve,
But, believe me, there are things in here
You'll find hard to believe.

Pass it on, pass it on –
But don't reveal your source.
Would your doctor or solicitor
Betray you? No, of course!
You might have heard a rumour –
That's all right, but it's essential
That you keep it hugger mugger
Hush-hush, highly confidential.

Don't ask me where I got it from.
Let's say a little bird
Has told me that it's genuine,
So do not breathe a word.
Potentially, it's dynamite –
Incredible but true.
So can we keep it quiet please
And strictly entre nous.

But pass it on, pass it on!
I'm sure you'll realise

The strategy behind it –
To discredit them with lies.
You've heard a rumour. OK?
For in my line it's essential
That we keep this hugger mugger
Hush-hush, highly confidential.

It's restricted information,
So I know you'll understand
That discussion of this document
Is absolutely banned.
It's more than my career is worth
If this should ever leak,
But if you promise mum's the word
I'll let you take a peak.

So pass it on, pass it on!
But don't say I told you so.
My friends all think it's something
That the public ought to know.
Just say you've heard a rumour –
That's enough! For it's essential
That we keep it hugger mugger,
Hush-hush, highly confidential.

It's important that the contents here
Should never be made known,
So when you tell the *Daily Mail*
Use someone else's phone.
As to who the author is
You'll have to make a guess.
He's a friend of you-know-who and,
By the way, that's his address.

Before I let you have this copy
Promise to agree
That this is unattributable
As it's Section D.
You've never had this conversation.
Never, I repeat!
Now excuse me for I really must get
Back to Downing Street.

REGATTA NATTER

Hey-ho! It's out with the flannels
The white shoes and boater of straw.
On with the motley and yellow striped blazer!
Come down and lend us an oar!
Hey-ho – Range Rover and Bentley
To Henley-on-Thames we all hasten.
From Marlow to Oxford, the wind's in the willows.
The hamper's from Fortnum and Mason.

Cucumber sandwiches, strawberries and cream
And Pimms No. 1 for our tea.
Most of the women appear to be dressed
With a view to appear on Page Three.
Gucci and Liberty's flying about
All desperately trying to chat
The nearest available Turnbull and Asser
Who looks like an aristocrat.

Hey-ho for all the Sloane Rangers
Sipping their iced lemonade,
Flitting like butterflies down on the Thames –
The *Country Life/Tatler* brigade.
Let's go! Get out of the city!
Life's dull with all work and no play.
And it's hey-ho for all of the secretaries
Stuck in the office all day.

Nouveau riche punters in hired cabin cruisers
Who lower the tone of the place –
They spend all their time on their mobiles and laptops
Then ask you 'Who won the last race?'
There are hot dogs and hamburgers, onions and ketchup
And paper cups full of warm beer,
Selfies and over-priced souvenir programmes.
We really don't want all that here.

Hey-ho! We don't watch the racing.
It's just a delightful day out.
We've never been able to fathom
What all of this rowing's about.
Oh no – we don't go to Henley
To see all these chappies in boats.
The idea of the thing is to see how much bubbly
We're able to toss down our throats.

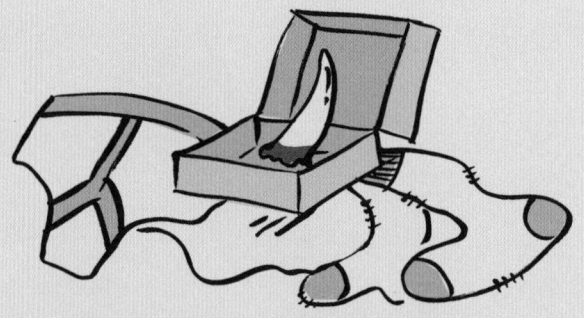

Bran Tub

TRESPUSSING

Excuse me, but please would you move from my bed?
I have told you again and again.
I don't know how often it has to be said:
You're a pussy and I'm a Great Dane.

You've got your own basket. It's over there. See?
It's the small one that's next to the sink.
When I ask you to shift I expect you to go
And not to just sit there and blink.

My mistress and I have come back from our walk
And I don't mind admitting I'm whacked.
I want to lie down. Are you deaf? Are you blind?
Are you getting a cat cataract?

I can't possibly fit into your little bunk
And don't think for a moment I'll try.
You're a dog in the manger with all of this space –
Now don't be a nuisance. Shoo-fly!

The trouble with you and the rest of your ilk
Is your self-possessed, indolent pose.
The last time you did this to me, I recall,
You spat at me, then scratched my nose.
I've heard people say that in fact you're a stray
And they found you in some kind of slum.
Well, I'm one up on you for my blood's royal blue.
Yes, I am a pedigree, chum.

You're the laziest, lousiest cat I have met.
Every dog that I know would concur.
You are not at all nice, you can't even catch mice
But just sleep and eat, scratch things and purr.
I've had quite enough, so just listen! Ruff! Ruff!
Grrr! Harooo! You heard what I said.
I will bark in your face till you're in your own place.
For the last time, get out of my bed!

* * *

Now I'm in the dog-house for making a noise
You over-fed, under-bred brat.
Dear oh dear, the indignity I must endure
Of cohabiting here with a cat.

But every Great Dane has his day, as they say.
It's been worth every minute, by heck,
When the mistress came in and without further ado
Threw you out by the scruff of your neck!

Sir Sacheverell Sitwell was the younger brother of Sir Osbert Sitwell and Dame Edith Sitwell. I meant no disrespect when I wrote this in 1986 – it was just his unusual Christian name that appealed to me. I wanted to see how many words beginning with 'Sh' I could fit around 'Sacheverell'.

SIR SACHEVERELL SITWELL
(1897-1988)

A message has come, Sir Sacheverell –
There's a shindig at Seamus's shack,
A reception! And so
Shall I say that you'll show
If I chauffeur Sir's Chevrolet back?

Oh yes, Sir, I'm sure they'll serve sherry
And a shot of some sherbet, perhaps.
Should you wish, there'll be brandy,
Champagne, Schweppes and shandy
Or should I suggest, Sir, some schnapps?

Sir Sacheverell, shut up the chateau.
They say that it's chic, this shebeen.
There'll be sheds full of shicker,
A mishmash of liquor
From schooners of scotch to poteen.

(LATER)

We should shove off soon now, Sir Sacheverell.
You've despatched rather more than a schluck.
In fact you've had several
Too many, Sacheverell.
You're smashed, sloshed and sozzled, you schmuck.

HYMN FOR TODAY

(Sung to 'Ellacombe' or any 7.6.7.6.D metre hymn tune)

O Jesus, how I love you!
To you my love I send!
I hope that you will love me too
And be my Facebook friend.
I worship and adore you
Nearly more than words can say.
I got that from a greetings card
I bought the other day.

I must admit theology
Is not my strongest card.
These words I write could never be
Mistaken for the Bard.
It simply doesn't matter though!
I know He doesn't mind
Because He died to save me
And He's merciful and kind.

I'll now compose a tune for this
And as I wash your feet
I'll think of something catchy
With a poppy kind of beat.
It won't be very difficult
Or challenging to sing –
A kindergarten, clappy
Eurovision sort of thing.

Those oldie hymns my parents sing
I do not understand.
An organ's too old-fashioned
So my friends have formed a band.
We pretend we're all on telly
Which we know we'll never be,
But Lord Jesus is our rock star
So that's good enough for me.

So get out your recorders
Your guitars and tambourines!
Pretend you're back in Sunday School
And not yet in your teens.
Then sing this song to Jesus –
Yes, just sing and dance and clap! –
And you'll be one of several thousand
Singing pseudo-Christian crap.

THE DECISION MAKERS

Let's have a committee
Then write a report.
Let's have an investigation,
Then take it to court,
Set up a commission,
Take legal advice.
Then we can blame it on somebody else –
Surely, it's worth the price?

Let's have a White Paper,
Let's kick it about,
Let's decide not to decide
And leave some room for doubt.
Set up an enquiry –
It's only common sense –
Then we can wash our hands of it
And sit firmly on the fence.

After the horse has bolted,
Let's meet up and discuss
What the hell we ought to have done
And make a belated fuss.
Let's draft a proposal
And have a long debate,
Then come to the wrong decision –
As long as it's far too late.

Let's set up a quango!
Let's do some research!
Let's all feel important
And let's involve the Church.
Establish a Royal Commission
Which we'll all ignore
And keep our findings secret
In case we've broken the law.

Let's make an announcement
And run it up the pole.
Better find a scape-goat, though,
In case we're in a hole.
Select a select committee –
A warm and friendly bunch –
But let's not make our minds up yet.
Besides, it's time for lunch.

* * *

A Scotsman called Robert the Bruce
Had a tartan of yellow and puce.
His friends asked "Oh why does
He talk to those spiders?
D'ye think Bruce has got a screw loose?"

* * *

"Nurse Sunshine Of Bedfordshire Weds"
Ran the headline I saw here at Fred's.
And the young lady's name
Was Miss Rosemary Frame.
On the ward she is sweet "Rose of Beds".

* * *

The limerick (below) was written for a book of limericks by 'personalities from the worlds of television, sport, films and politics' collected by the actor Tom Baker. The paperback, published in 1984, was called *The Boy Who Forgot to Grow Down*, with royalties going to the charity Help a Child to See.

A train driver living in Crewe
Went down with a bad dose of 'flu.
He snuffled and wheezed
And, of course, when he sneezed
He went 'AH-choo choo choo choo! Ah-CHOO!'

* * *

A sea-bird on the rocky shore
Was wandering all alone
When he saw a sea-girl maiden
With a face much like his own.
He squawked and asked her if she'd be
A sea-bird wife and mother.
She answered, "Yes, for one good tern
I know deserves another".

* * *

UNCLE FRED

I've had a few laughs in my lifetime –
I've laughed and I've laughed till I cried.
But the funniest thing I remember
Was the day that my Uncle Fred died.
He was a real bastard.

* * *

THERE'S A PARTRIDGE ON MY CHIMNEY

There's a partridge on my chimney.
He's been there about a week.
He says that I invited him.
Of all the blooming cheek!
He wakes me every morning
With a horrid, spiteful cry
And I can't get back to sleep again
No matter how I try.
He makes a frightful racket
Like a rooster – only worse.
And when I hear that partridge cry
My goodness, how I curse.
I toss and turn and wonder
Should I call the chimney sweep.
He'd knock off any partridges
That dare disturb my sleep.

There's a partridge on my chimney
And he simply will not move.
It is really most annoying
So if things do not improve
I shall get out pen and paper,
Write a letter to *The Times*
And let the nation know just how
I feel about his crimes.

For although he knows he's trespassing
He doesn't feel remorse.
And at five tomorrow morning
He will still be there of course.
I threw a rubber ball at him –
I'd knock him off with luck –
But blow me if I didn't see
That wretched partridge duck!
I've shouted at him, called him names
And cried "Please fly away!"
But he doesn't take the hint
And comes back every single day.
He perches on that chimney top
As if he owns the place.
I tell you, I'd be angry
If I met him face to face.

I'd say, "Listen, Mr. Partridge,
If you really must sit there
Will you kindly put a sock in it –
Your singing drives me spare!"
You think this has a happy end?
Well, sadly, it does not.
I shot that blooming partridge
And put him in a pot.
I know that all my vegan friends
Will say that this is frightful,
But, honestly, smoked partridge
As a dish is quite delightful.

WHAT IS THE POINT OF A NIPPLE?

What is the point of a nipple?
You cover them up with your vest!
They could be on your arm
On your knees or your palm
But instead they're attached to your chest.

What is the point of a nipple?
I really don't know why they're there.
I haven't a clue
What the silly things do –
And Dad's are all covered in hair.

MY GRANDMA WEARS A PETTICOAT

My grandma wears a petticoat.
I've seen her put it on.
She also wears elastic panties
"'Cos my tummy's gone".
I wonder what she means by this?
'Cos once I saw her bare
And I saw her tummy for myself.
Her tummy is still there!

I'd like to wear a petticoat.
My grandma's is so pretty.
She wears a dress that hides it up –
I think that's such a pity.
Why grandma wears a petticoat
Is difficult to say,
But she told me Grandpa bought it for her
On their wedding day.

GRANDMA'S GOT A TIGER'S TOOTH

Grandma's got a tiger's tooth.
She keeps it in a box
In the corner of a drawer
With grandpa's underwear and socks.

How grandma came to have the tooth
Is a tale too long to tell,
But when the tiger had its tooth pulled out
It must have hurt like hell.

"And did the tiger bite you, Grandma?
Did it do you any harm?"
"Oh yes, my dear," she said. "That's why
I've only got one arm."

* * *

THE URBAN DISTRICT PLANNER

I'm an urban district planner
Of a forward-looking bent,
I'm practical and ruthless
With a lack of sentiment.
When dwelling units I design
There's no place like a home
That's double-glazed, pre-fabricated,
Melamite and chrome…

That Grade Two listed building
At the corner of the street
Is an eye-sore, it's collapsing
And, besides, it's obsolete.
King George the Third was on the throne
When the house was built –
It's got no central heating
And the wall's inclined to tilt.
Perhaps it looked all right
When it was in a market town –
But I'm an urban district planner
And I'm going to pull it down.

There's a Jacobean mansion here
That's quite beyond repair.
Unfortunately, though, there are
Some people living there.

I don't let that disturb me
When I go to sleep at night –
It's absolutely perfect
For a supermarket site.
Demolition Orders over-rule
The National Trust
And before you've said 'Hey presto!'
It will be a pile of dust.

Give me a shopping centre!
I can proudly claim.
Every one that I've designed
Looks totally the same.
Who needs imagination
In a job like mine?
It's quicker and far cheaper
When it's bland and anodyne.
Let's make it 1980s
Concrete slabs and glass.
Chop down that row of trees
And tear up all the grass.
Bulldoze the countryside,
Hedgerow and lane!
You'll waste your time protesting
With your anti-house campaign.
No use trying to stop me.
Your sort never understands
That it's going to happen anyway –
When money changes hands.

Love and Loss

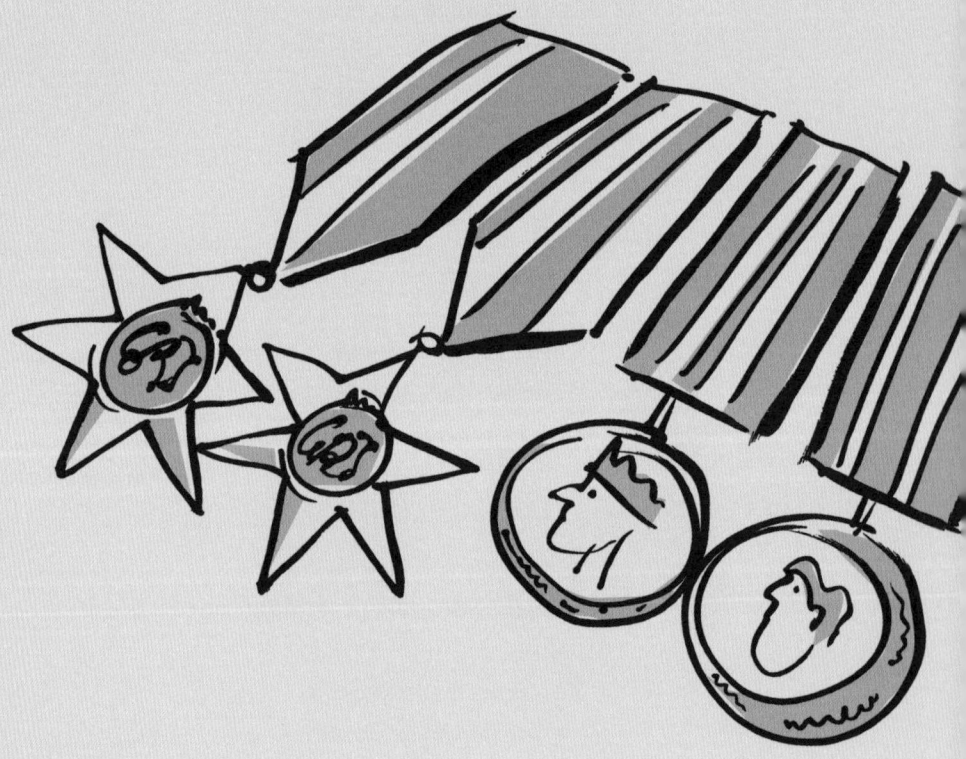

DAD GOT ALL HIS MEDALS OUT TODAY

Dad got all his medals out today.
I hadn't seen them, oh, for years and years.
When I was just a kid, I caught him polishing them once
And, do you know, his eyes were filled with tears.
"Go on then, run along," he said.
"I'll be up in a minute and I'll tuck you into bed."

That night he told me all about the War –
Winston Churchill and Tobruk and Vera Lynn,
About the blackouts and the Blitz, the indomitable Brits.,
Yanks and tanks and how we took it on the chin.
He told me how he learnt to fire a rifle,
How he watched the German bombers in the skies,
How he'd done his bit for King and Country and the time he saw
His closest friend wiped out before his very eyes,
The U-Boats and the Spitfires and machine guns,
The deserts and the crowds on VE Day,
But when I asked him how he got his medals,
Well, the strange thing is my father wouldn't say.

Dad got all his medals out today.
He's going to a celebration 'do'.
The boys from the battalion are dining out again
On the memories and tales of World War Two.
"Not many of us left these days," he said.
Shades of Shakespeare and of 'Gentlemen in England now abed'.

"You'll never understand about the War.
You kids today don't know what it was like.
The memories remain – Alvar Liddell and Alamein,
Glenn Miller, Goering, Himmler, Monty, Ike,
Mussolini and the Russians and the rations,
And all of Churchill's 'Blood, toil, tears and sweat',
The BBC and ITMA and Normandy and Hitler
Are the things that I'm unlikely to forget."
So today Dad put his medals on again
On the anniversary of VE Day.
He got the D.S.O. and bar – a row of others, too.
How he got them, though, he's never going to say.

WHERE ONCE

Where once there was a meadow
There's now, I'm sad to say,
A queue of stationary cars
They call a motorway.

Where once there was a hedgerow
With every shade of green
There now are splintered sticks the council
Flayed with a machine.

Where once there was a grass verge
With flowers and weeds galore
There's now a pavement to conform
To local safety law.

Where once there was a forest
They have cleared a picnic spot
With a car park and a snack bar
And a crèche and God knows what.

Where once from my back window
There were views to captivate
Of woods and fields and distant hills
There's now a new estate.

Where once there stood an oak tree
There's now an empty space.
Four hundred years it stood there –
Four hundred to replace.

COUNTING THE STARS ALONE

I've been a fool over you, I admit.
And the way that you treated me hurt just a bit.
Leading me up the garden path
Was easy as could be.
Now I can't find my way back home
Without you here with me.
I reached out to the sky for my prize
And all that I got was a packet of lies,
Once more to reap the whirlwind
After the wind I'd sown,
Lying here waiting for daybreak,
Counting the stars alone.

I forgot all the lessons I'd learned,
So it's not so surprising my fingers were burned.
Catching my breath each time I saw you
Swept me off my feet,
Turning my back on danger signs
When my heart skipped a beat.
Now I run through the things that we said –
All those passionate truths are now clichés instead –
Watching my flight of wonder
Sink to the depths like stone,
Waiting for you and daybreak,
Counting the stars alone.

THE MAN IN THE OLD TUXEDO

In the Mediterranean sunshine
Under skies of an azure blue,
I've returned to the tiny village
Which I stumbled across with you.
So I thought that I'd write a letter
To tell you that, since we came,
There's nothing to show
It was long, long ago,
For everything's just the same.

There's the man in the old tuxedo
Singing songs to a small guitar.
And I stopped still and stared
At the room that we shared
Across from the local bar.

For the man in the old tuxedo
Unwittingly casts his spell
And I look through a haze
To those long-distant days,
And without you it hurts like hell.

* * *

I went down to the silver sand dunes
And the beach where we lazed each day,
And I know if you'd made this journey
Then you'd never have gone away.
For I went to the scented pine wood
And looked up at the stars above
And I heard from afar
In the night the guitar
At the place where we first made love.

Yes, the man in the old tuxedo
Sings the songs that he sang before.
It brings back, so it seems,
You and me in my dreams
By that Mediterranean shore.
And half of me wants to be here
And half of me wants to go,
For the way the guy sings
And the memories he brings
Without you here hurt me so.

OCTOBER SUNSHINE

Oh October sunshine
No brighter than the moon
Dying with our love up in the sky,
Just a few short months ago
You shone out bright all day,
But oh October sunshine
You're old and cold and grey.

Oh October sunshine,
The summer days have gone.
They've vanished like the love we used to have.
Mustn't let it linger on.
You know you needn't stay
And oh October sunshine
You're old and cold and grey.

Where have you gone to?
Thought you'd shine on me all year.
How could you have the heart
To disappear…?

Oh October sunshine
You're looking kind of sad,
But you and I will live to laugh again.
Just a few short memories
The rain will wash away.
And oh October sunshine
You're old and cold and grey.

THE LONG GOODBYE

It's been lovely being with you
But I've really got to fly.
I have to go, so cheerio,
I'll take my leave. Bye bye...

It's time to slip off and make an exit,
Though I can hardly bear to tear myself away.
Yes, I must flit. I quit! That's it!
Such a shame, 'cos I should dearly love to stay.

It's been a pleasure, but *tempus fugit*.
It is getting rather late, so au revoir.
I must press on. I'll see you all anon,
So 'bye for now! Ta-ta!

I certainly don't want to hurt your feelings,
But "Goodness me, it's nearly half-past one!"
While diplomacy and tact
Can scarcely hide the fact
[*Yawning*] "I can't remember when I last had so much fun".

So let's weigh anchor and skedaddle,
Let's beat it, hop it, scram and fly the nest,
Let's saddle up, get out of here
And take a well-earned rest.

* * *

Parting, so they say, is such sweet sorrow,
But I'm knackered and my throat is rather rough.
Would you mind if I withdraw before you ask for an encore?
Because, frankly, I've had just about enough...

I've got to dash now! The taxi's waiting!
I must beetle, buzz or be off and vamoose!
I can't remain! I have to catch a train –
At least, I'm using that as my excuse.

Auf Wiedersehen, dear! Adios, amigos!
I hope by now there's not the slightest doubt
I've reached the end. Goodbye, my friend.
No, please don't move – I'll find my own way out.

We'll meet again but don't know where or when yet.
So very glad at last our paths have crossed.
We'll keep a welcome in the Rhonddha,
Absence makes the heart grow fonder,
But, just for now, get lost!

Arrivederci! So nice to meet you.
As I leave the stage and take a final bow
I wave a fond farewell! Adieu!
Bon voyage and ciao!
It's been lovely being with you
But I've simply got to fly.
I have to go,
So cheerio,
Goodbye...

Goodbye...

Goodbye...

Goodbye...

Goodbye!